Dave Peck's
CHAMPIONSHIP RACQUETBALL SYSTEM:
LEARNING TO PLAY BY THE NUMBERS

by Dave Peck with Armen Keteyian

Edited by Jerry Day

A Fireside Book
Published by Simon & Schuster, Inc.
New York

A Fireside Book
Published by Simon & Schuster, Inc.
Simon & Schuster Building
Rockefeller Center
1230 Avenue of the Americas
New York, New York 10020

FIRESIDE and colophon are registered trademarks of Simon & Schuster, Inc.

Designed by Stanley S. Drate/Folio Graphics Co. Inc.

Manufactured in the United States of America

10 9 8 7 6 5 4 3 2 1

Library of Congress Cataloging in Publication Data

Peck, Dave.
  Dave Peck's Championship racquetball system.

  "A Fireside book."
  1. Racquetball. I. Keteyian, Armen. II. Day,
Jerry. III. Title. IV. Title: Championship racquetball
system.
GV1003.34.P43 1985   796.34′3   85-14442
ISBN 0-670-49434-1

CONTENTS

DAVE PECK'S

CHAMPIONSHIP RACQUETBALL SYSTEM:

LEARNING TO PLAY BY THE NUMBERS

1
PHILOSOPHY AND
INTRODUCTION

*R*acquetball's lifeblood, the power behind its popularity, has always stemmed from the simplicity of the sport. Simple equipment. Simple surroundings. Simple rules. Simple sweat. Even those with average or below-average athletic skills can enjoy batting the ball around for a half-hour or so, eventually carrying a sense of accomplishment off the court. Yet soon enough, after this simplicity comes the confusion, the awkwardness, the difficulties tied to learning "how to play the game," improving beyond sweat and into the science of the sport. And, to be honest, in my amateur days and now as a professional player and instructor, I've found a simple reason: Many of those teaching the sport—fundamental strokes, proper positioning, knowing what shot to hit at what time—aren't truly adept at breaking it down mechanically, bit by bit, showing a student the rock-bottom basics of the game. Part of the problem is the relative youth of our sport. In golf or baseball there are highly organized associations that teach fundamentals and offer coaching and guidance, but for the most part we racquetball players have to learn on our own.

In clubs all over this country I've watched instructors—fine players themselves—tell students to "hit the ball like this" with only a rare explanation of what "this" actually is. And because racquetball is not a sport in which one gets much on-the-job training—it's too reactive and instinctive—beginning and intermediate players often leave the sport, frustrated in their attempts to improve beyond the "flailing away" stage.

Yet racquetball is a very popular sport in the United States and is gaining support. By industry estimates, there are more than 11 million players in this country with some 50,000 beginners entering the sport each year. It's my belief that virtually every one of those 11 million could benefit from a strong dose of the fundamentals. That's where I hope to help.

In this book you'll find a simple, systematic approach to both shot-making and strategy. Most important, you'll learn *how* to hit a forehand and backhand before you learn *where* to hit them. So many instructors suggest strategy and angles and passes without ever mentioning much more about the forehand and backhand than "stay low and snap your wrist at impact." That's because they haven't broken down the swing. They can blast the ball and move it around the court, but they don't know *why.* To me, it's important you learn everything there is to know about the letters A and B before even worrying about C through Z.

My system is not something I pulled out of a hat. It's the product of my own search for simplicity, a search that started fairly late in life. I didn't begin playing racquetball until I was nineteen, and while today I'm known as a fun-loving good ol' boy from Texas (which I am) I also take great pride in my knowledge of the mechanics of this sport. I grew up a pretty fair athlete—a four-year starter at linebacker in high school, state finalist in wrestling, diver—and I played freshman football at the University of Texas–El Paso for a spell, but when I started playing recquetball (my sister taught me) there was nobody around to say what was technically right and wrong. So I've developed my own system, one, I think, that's proved quite effective. I joined the tour during the 1978-79 season and was named Rookie of the Year. Since then I've consistently ranked in the top four, and during the 1982 season I was named Player of the Year by *Racquetball Illustrated Magazine,* won the national title, and was ranked No. 1. My system has also helped younger players from my hometown of El Paso, and four of my students have won national age-group titles, including my younger brother Gregg, now one of the finest players in the game.

Of course, I understand it's not feasible or desirable for everyone to attempt to be a champion, certainly not on a national level. Racquetball is a workout and, according to a recent study, a darn good one. You burn more calories per minute in our sport (13.7 for men and 10.4 for women) than you do in cycling, handball, or tennis. Yet beyond exercise it's important, before reading much farther, to define your objectives. Okay, you don't want to win the national fifty-and-over title, but you would like to climb up the club challenge ladder, or beat your boss at least once before you retire. You should understand that some of your

progress is dictated by genetics—this is, after all, a sport that places a premium on hand-eye coordination, footwork, and speed—but don't limit yourself; don't be discouraged by nay-sayers like those who told me I was "too big" to be a pro player. Don't let others influence how you feel about yourself and this game. Go for it.

A student in my summer racquetball camp once told me, "It doesn't matter whether I win or lose." Doesn't it? Of course it does. Not caring about winning or losing comes from never winning. Win once and you'll want to experience that feeling again; it's that kind of drive that helps you master the mechanics of this sport. But let's not kid ourselves—we're all going to lose sometimes. That fine, because it's the lessons you learn from defeat, lessons you never experience with victory, that help you become a big winner later on.

Let me explain. Raymond, a superstar in the junior ranks who won a national title at age thirteen, quit playing six years after that victory. He was a tremendous athlete, so gifted he won matches on ability alone. But he had no practice habits and little dedication. Soon people he had crushed early in his career started turning the tables, and Raymond just couldn't handle it. He had never been exposed to losing, and instead of fighting to improve—learning from his losses—he left the game completely. The moral of that story is fairly self-evident.

I hope you'll find this book is a bread-and-butter approach to the game. Beginning or low-intermediate players stand to gain the most, but it wouldn't hurt a lot of A and Open players to review the basics and incorporate my simple "By the Numbers" system into their games.

What is By the Numbers? It means exactly what it says—racquetball shots based on hitting from one numbered area of the court to another. The court is divided vertically into zones based upon spots on the front wall, back wall, and service area.

The numbers along the front wall read 0-½-1-1½-2-2½-3-3½-4 from left to right. They are numbered the same along both the back wall and the service zone. The abbreviations FW, BW, and S in front of the numbers indicate which surface is meant. Front wall extreme left corner would be FW 0. Thus for a forehand drive serve, we would simply instruct a right-handed player to hit the shot from S 3 (serving area 3, the right-center of the box) to FW 3½ (or far right about 1 foot from the wall). To hit a crosscourt pass from deep in the court, the advice would be BW 3½ to FW 2½.

This numbering system takes the guesswork out of shot-making and increases reaction speed. As play develops you don't have to file through the index cards of your mind, thinking, "Now what shot do I hit in this situation and where do I hit it?" In short order you'll see how simple and systematic it really is . . . if you just follow the numbers.

(1)

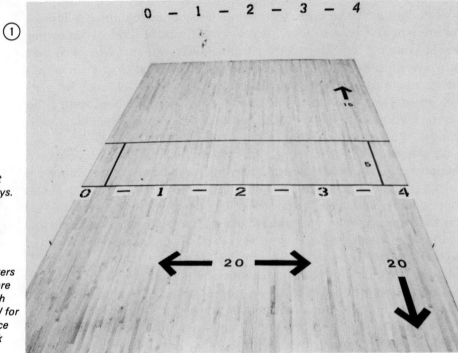

BY THE NUMBERS: *It means just what it says. The front wall, the service area, and the back wall (not shown here) are all divided vertically into areas numbered 0 to 4. Letters before the numbers are used to indicate which surface is meant—FW for front wall, S for service area, and BW for back wall.*

2

THE GAME AND
ITS HISTORY

THE GAME

Racquetball is generally played on an enclosed court (an outdoor, three-wall game is popular in California) that is 40 feet long, 20 feet high, and 20 feet wide. Most indoor facilities have hardwood floors and white plaster walls, but in many clubs there are generally a few "glass-enclosed" exhibition courts for viewing pro matches or tournament-type play.

While squash uses a dead ball and a long racquet with a small hitting surface, racquetball employs a lively black or blue ball and shorter racquets, generally 18¼ inches in length. The court is divided in half by a "short line" 20 feet from the front wall, and there is a "service line" 5 feet in front of the short line. Lines 18 inches from each side wall connect the service line and short line and mark off the service boxes, in which a server's partner must stand during a doubles match. The remaining space between the service line and short line is the service zone.

The game begins with a person serving from the service zone, with his opponent at least 5 feet behind the service line. A ball can hit any number of walls during a rally, but must touch the front wall before it hits the floor; if not, it's a "skip" and the opponent's serve. Shots cannot bounce twice on the floor. A point or serve is won by a player when his opponent fails to hit the front wall, "skips" the ball, or lets it bounce twice on the floor.

The server must bounce the ball once in the service zone, then hit it with the racquet toward the front wall. Should you strike the side wall, floor, or ceiling before hitting the front wall, it's an out serve, and you lose your serve. If you make another type of error, such as hitting the back wall on the fly with a serve that's a bit too strong, it's a fault, and you are entitled to one more serve.

Return-of-serve rules forbid a player from hitting a serve until it passes the short line. Contact is usually made after the first bounce, but if you see the opportunity to pick off a soft lob serve, particularly to your opponent's strong side, you should do so—provided it has passed the receiving line, 5 feet behind the short line. A returner can use any combination of walls (the ceiling is fine), provided the ball doesn't first hit the floor before striking the front wall (called a "skip").

Generally, only a server (or serving side in doubles) can win a point, although in some Women's Professional Racquetball Tournaments the women play under rules which allow both players to score. Points are won by serving an "ace"—an unreturnable serve—or by taking a rally. And while the "magic" number of winning points has shifted from 21 to 15 to even 11 in recent years, most racquetball matches are the best two of three games with the third game played to an 11-point or 15-point "tiebreaker," depending on your scoring system.

Rules also stipulate play should be stopped for a "hinder," the unintentional or intentional interference with one's opponent during play. Because racquetball is played in such confined quarters, especially when four people occupy the space, hinders do occur. If you accidentally move into your opponent's arm swing or shooting zone, consider it a hinder and replay the point. If you purposely move into those areas, shame on you—it's an "avoidable hinder" and you lose either the point or the serve.

A "screen" is an obstruction of vision. Basically a screen is called when you obscure your opponent's view of the ball—moving late in his shooting zone, or worse, not moving at all. The same rules apply as for hinders.

A short history lesson on the sport:

500 B.C. Reliefs on the Wall of Themistocles depict men playing with a small round object.

1555 The game of court tennis is played in France, using a strung racquet with a short handle, almost identical in shape to modern racquetball racquets.

1757 Court tennis is played in England. Today the game still employs a racquetball-shaped racquet with a shortened handle.

1850 Squash is invented at the Harrow School in England.

1940s Paddleball increases in popularity and is played by the U.S. Armed Forces and at YMCAs and other community centers across America.

1949 Joe Sobek, a tennis and squash pro from Greenwich, Connecticut, brings a shortened tennis racquet into a handball court, merging the game of tennis with an indoor four-wall court. The game is called paddle rackets, later racquetball. It spreads to YMCAs across the country.

1962 Bud Held, former world record holder in the javelin, experiments with the first aluminum tennis racquet.

1968-69 The International Racquetball Association is formed, standardizing rules, courts, and equipment for the first time.

1969 Bud Muehleisen asks Held to make him an aluminum racquetball racquet. Muehleisen wins the first international championship with it.

1970-71 By this time there are 50,000 racquetball players in the U.S.A. A pro tour is organized.

1978 Now there are 8 million racquetball players in the country and more than 800 court clubs and 17,000 individual courts.

1979 Participation grows to nearly 10 million, racquetball breaks into television, and corporate sponsors begin to fund nationwide pro tours. Juniors programs start to develop.

1980 The Women's Professional Racquetball Association is formed, as the growth pattern in the sport begins to level off.

1984 After a period of moderate growth, player numbers increase to the 12 million mark with about 50,000 new players each year. In four years the WPRA has expanded from 50 to 400 members, and pro tours for both sexes continue to attract interest around the country.

3
GEARING UP

*O*ne of the things I love about racquetball is that you don't need a major credit card to play. Outside of a racquet and a ball, the rest of the gear can be found in anybody's bedroom: T-shirt, socks, a pair of gym shorts, and court shoes. Eye guards are strongly recommended but at this stage of the sport's development still optional, as are gloves, wristbands, and headbands.

THE RACQUET

The evolution of racquet technology has changed dramatically in the last five years. Once the only choice was wood or aluminum. Then racquets of injection-molded fiberglass and graphite were developed. Now racquets of composite compounds like boron and kevlar are on the market, and state-of-the-art products like Ektelon's CBK Racquet retail for $175. However, for both beginning and intermediate players, racquets are available for from $30 to $75. You can also rent racquets from court clubs while deciding which kind is best suited to your interest and playing style.

When you do decide to buy, be cautious. While cheaper racquets are fine, they are, as a rule, generally more "flexible," giving players a greater margin for error. That would include all aluminum and most graphite models. When you move into the high-priced models, racquet frames are generally much stiffer and have a reduced "sweet spot."

Don't be talked into buying a high-priced racquet until your game is ready for it. Shop around, remembering the two most important elements are grip size and weight. Ektelon now offers an oversized "macro" racquet built along the lines of those popularized by Prince in tennis. It's 2 inches longer and 3 inches wider than standard models, with 30 square inches more string surface, and it weighs only 245 grams. But for the most part, your decisions will be among standard models.

WHAT TO LOOK FOR

First, the grip. Make sure it's small enough for ample wrist action but not so small it moves around in your hand. One of the biggest fallacies in the sport is that large men feel they need thick-handled racquets. It's actually just the opposite. Grip sizes run between super-small (3 $^{11}/_{16}$ inches) and large (4 $^1/_2$ inches). Most men find comfort in extra-small (3 $^{15}/_{16}$ inches) or small (4 $^1/_8$ inches) grips, while women find super-small or small grips suit them best.

Length: The standard measure for most players is 18¼ inches. It's much easier to control a racquet this size than a longer one. Still, you may want to take a look at the "oversized" models, particularly in the early stages of your game's development.

Weight: The compromise here is about 245 grams for most people, though racquets do run from 230 to 255 grams. You don't want your racquet so light you can't generate any force, but at the same time, you don't want to burden yourself with excess baggage in a game that depends on your ability to execute.

Stiffness: As mentioned, the standard rule is the higher-priced the model, the stiffer the racquet. A racquet's stiffness translates to power, but it also allows less margin for error.

Frame: This is where the most advances have been made in the sport. Composite racquets made of space-age materials, racquets like the Ektelon 250G or CBK, are finely tuned instruments of graphite fibers, boron, aluminum alloys, stainless steel, "chopped" graphite, and fiberglass.

OTHER EQUIPMENT

- Wrist thongs are mandatory, so make sure one is attached to your racquet. Make sure you use it when you play.
- Gloves have become more popular. Lightweight models made of such exotic material as cabretta sheepskin keep your hand dry, restricting the racquet's movement at impact.
- Eye guards are used less than they should be. For safety's sake, take a good look at the various products. Manufacturers now produce eye guards in all shapes and sizes with an accent on fashion, so there's really no excuse for not wearing them.
- Your feet take a big pounding in this sport, so it's wise to protect them. Before getting serious about the sport, buy a good pair of court shoes made to take a lot of stopping and starting. Also load up on white socks and try to wear two pairs when playing.
- As far as the rest of your wardrobe is concerned, my suggestion is to wear what's comfortable. If you like playing in clothes designed by Ralph Lauren, so be it. There's plenty of "fashionwear" or "active-wear" on the market. The racquetball company I'm sponsored by, Ektelon, makes a beautiful, functional line of activewear. Of course, there's also nothing wrong in showing up in a T-shirt and gym shorts. It's all a matter of personal taste.

4
THE FOREHAND
AND BACKHAND

*T*he history and philosophy classes are over. It's time for basic training. But as any drill instructor will tell you, before attacking your opponent, be prepared. In racquetball, even before learning the how-tos of the forehand and backhand strokes, there are a couple of other lessons to learn.

THE READY POSITION

One of the most common mistakes in a racquet sport, be it tennis, squash, or racquetball, is not being ready to hit a shot. In clubs around the country I regularly see a ball entering a player's "power zone," an area I'll describe in a second, while the racquet is down at the player's knees. It doesn't do any good down there. By the time you bring it up into the zone where you contact the ball, the ball has zipped past. Of course, you can inhibit your game by bringing your elbow up (the beginning of your forehand stroke) too soon. Think for a second. How easy is it to sprint around the court with your elbow in the air? Not very. Lifting an elbow eliminates the use of an arm to run. A faster, more efficient manner is to begin to bring your elbow up when the ball begins to come up 2 or 3 feet from your power zone.

And when you're anticipating a play, or in the middle of a point, stay prepared by keeping your feet a shoulder width apart. Remain on the balls of your feet as much as possible. Watch any of the greats in sports which require agility and foot movement—Jimmy Connors in tennis, Pele in soccer—and you'll see that they play on the balls of their feet. So should you.

THE SECOND-BOUNCE THEORY AND THE POWER-CONTROL STROKE

When the ball bounces off a wall or the ceiling just before you're about to hit it, it naturally rises to a peak before falling. You want to maneuver yourself so that the big toe of your front foot is where the ball would drop on its theoretical last bounce, i.e., where the ball would land if you decided not to hit the shot. When it does come down into this area, it's entering the power zone.

And just what is the power zone? I define it as the area from the big toe of the front foot to the inner thigh of the back leg. This is where you automatically snap your wrist (at the base of the zone) and where the transformation of weight from back to front occurs. It's critical to keep the ball in this zone, for even subtle shifts in the location of the ball invite error. For example, play the ball too far forward, beyond the big toe, and the ball hits too high off the front wall. Play it too far back, and you'll find yourself with a sudden case of the "skips." That's why quick feet and learning to read the angles are so important.

GETTING A GRIP: THE FOREHAND

The grip is one vital aspect that is universally ignored in the sport. Place your racquet perpendicular to the floor. Now shake hands with it, placing the heel of the racquet in the fleshy part of your palm. Don't grip it too far back, like a hammer; otherwise you'll lose control of the far end and find the racquet slipping out of your hand. Conversely, grip too low and you'll find yourself forced into squeezing the racquet much harder to keep control, and during long matches and tiebreakers, arm fatigue will lead you into making mistakes.

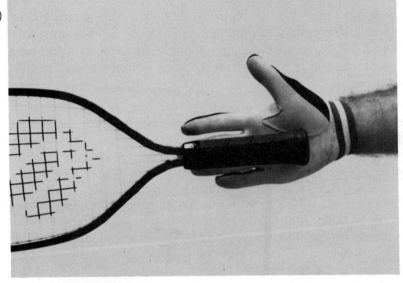

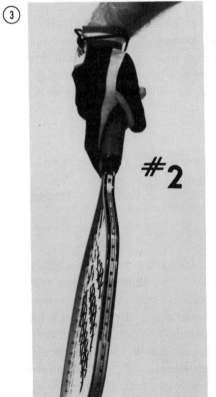

#2

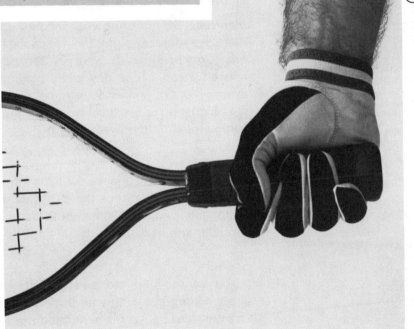

Ill. 2, 3:
*Proper hand position and
finger placement for the
forehand trigger grip.*

Ill. 4:
*The Number 2 Position
for the forehand trigger
grip.*

Now place your index finger on the back side of the racquet. This is called the trigger grip. It provides power, stability, and control. Now wrap your thumb around your middle finger. Check and see if the V of the racquet is in a No. 2 position, the middle of the racquet. A common mistake with this grip is grabbing all the way around the racquet, not utilizing the trigger.

THE STROKE

Step 1

Assume the ready position, pretending you're facing a side wall on the court. Now bring your elbow up, forearm parallel to the floor at a right angle from forearm to biceps. Keep your arm at shoulder height. If you're not sure what this should look like, make sure your shoulder and elbow form an L.

Incorrect: Do not bring your racquet up to a "salute" position. Keep it level, at shoulder height. Salutes cause two problems, the first of which one of my best friends, attorney Jerry Day, knows all too well. He gave himself a salute one day while playing in a tournament and cut his eyebrow open. And aside from being hazardous to your health, pulling the racquet up to eye level elongates the stroke and forces the elbow in, cutting maximum power and time.

Step 2

Only take the racquet back even with your shoulder. Pulling it farther back not only lengthens the stroke, cutting efficiency, but also, over a prolonged period of time, puts an incredible amount of strain on shoulder and back muscles.

Step 3

You want to step into the shot. Your front foot should end up angled about 45 degrees, with your back foot square. Why 45 degrees and not straight? Well, power is generated from pushing body weight forward, opening your hips, and getting hip rotation into the shot. It's vital to push off that back leg because it forces your hips to open and rotate. If your front leg remains even with your back, or worse, closes in, your hips lock and you can't reach your full power potential. A closed or even stance also forces the angle of your swing upward because your hips can't shift through. The 45-degree angle allows a lowering of your body

The Forehand Stroke: ready position.

*The Forehand Stroke:
incorrect salute position.*

Back shoulder set-up,

step,

into the ball. Most elbow injuries in racquetball are a result of not using legs, of trying to "muscle" the ball, relying too much on the arm, not legs.

Step 4

You must also drag the instep of your back foot. This will help keep you from skipping shots, as there is a tendency to stay up and lean over a shot. It's ironic how I discovered this. It wasn't until I hurt my leg badly in the Nationals in 1983, an injury which subsequently forced me to be concerned about pushing off, that I began to skip the ball. I finally traced it back to staying up on a shot and not sliding the back foot.

and follow-through.

THE ARM SWING

The arm swing and step should be almost simultaneous. The first movement is to lead with the elbow, pulling down like a pendulum, *not* into your side. Keep it 8 to 10 inches from your body and you should feel the tension on your shoulder when your elbow passes through on this arc.

It is at this tension point that you begin your extension. Elbow-extend, that's the thinking, and we do it for two reasons: to accelerate the racquet head coming into the ball, and to get the proper pronation/ extension of the arm to allow for maximum wrist snap.

When you do extend the racquet, force the face through square, perpendicular to the floor, like a sidearm pitch in baseball. As you follow

The Arm Swing: extending the elbow into the power zone.

Squaring off the racquet.

through, keep the racquet on the same plane as the shot, so the ball remains parallel to the floor. Some players' follow-throughs reach all the way up to their neck, and while this looks good in pictures, it automatically pushes your shot up a couple of inches, making re-kills a rather distinct possibility.

THE OTHER ARM

Well, you can always use it to grab the other guy on the court and throw him out of the way. Of course, you'll probably get warned or dinged a point for that move, since it's illegal. What to do with the arm is a problem many begin pondering after they hit themselves across the knuckles a couple of times. Basically, your free arm should rotate hard away from your body, pulling your hips open sharply and rotating your midsection. This helps generate power in the swing, but more important, in this case, it keeps your racquet level. The worst thing for your forehand is to try to guide a shot in your power zone. The secret to controlling the forehand, whether it's a killing shot, a crosscourt, or a

Rotating the opposite arm.

pass, is contacting the ball with the *same* stroke every single time. *The only thing that changes is where the ball is contacted in the power zone.* If you want to kill a shot, let the ball fall to just above court level. A crosscourt or pass should be contacted at knee level.

WHAT ABOUT WRIST ACTION?

Don't worry about it. It's automatic with your arm extension, as long as you assume the proper ready position, get that front foot angled at 45 degrees, and contact the ball squarely in the power zone.

CHECKLIST FOR THE FOREHAND

1. Place the racquet perpendicular to the floor, shaking hands so the heel is held in the fleshy part of your palm. Use the trigger grip, index finger on the back side of the racquet.

2. Facing the sidewall in the ready position, bring the elbow up, forearm parallel to the floor, arm and elbow at a right angle. Take the arm back only as far as the shoulder.
3. Step toward the area you're hitting at, with front foot angled 45 degrees and back foot square, then drag the back foot as you step into shot. Hit the ball off the inner thigh of the lead leg.
4. Arm swing and step should be simultaneous, elbow leading, staying 8 to 10 inches from the body.
5. Don't worry about wrist action, it's a natural part of the arm extension and proper contact in the power zone.
6. The racquet face should come through flat, follow-through remaining on the same plane as the shot. The opposite arm should act as counterweight, pulling open the hips, and helping to rotate the trunk.
7. Contact the ball with the same stroke on every forehand shot. The only variable is where the shot is contacted in the power zone.

THE BACKHAND

You see it in court clubs all over the country: Two players are battling it out, cracking out forehand after forehand, moving well, anticipating, drilling their serves, but then you notice a hole in the game the size of the state of Texas. *They can't hit a backhand.* Oh, they can keep the ball in play, with a timid, ill-placed shot that invariably ends too far up the front wall, but that's it. They can't put the ball away. They can't hit the shot accurately enough to move an opponent out of the key center-court position.

If you can't hit a good backhand, you begin to depend more and more on your forehand for point-winners, a strategy that leads directly into taking lower-percentage kill shots so that you can end a rally and not have to play a backhand any more than necessary. If you're playing someone with a strong backhand, it's also a strategy that often ends up costing you the match.

It shouldn't be so tough. In theory, the backhand is an easier stroke than the forehand because the fundamental arm movement and set-up are easier than that of the forehand. The backhand is only tougher because it is practiced and used less frequently, and therefore seems less natural to the majority of players. Once you overcome the mental hurdles associated with hitting the stroke, once you learn the fundamentals—the grip, the step, the elbow extension, the hip and shoulder rotation—you'll find what was once the missing link in your game has suddenly become the bridge which carries you into another dimension of play. The key is technique and timing. TnT. The result will be an explosive backhand.

If at all possible, you should always rotate your grip from the forehand to the backhand. This is easily done by moving your hand ¼ inch to the left on the racquet handle. This allows you to achieve the maximum amount of power with a minimal amount of effort. Also, when the arm is extended at contact, the rotation keeps your racquet face square at contact, negating the need to depend on what I call "the educated wrist," which simply means you have to think and concentrate on adjusting your wrist in the middle of a shot, something which requires maximum hand-eye coordination to hit the ball in the sweet spot of the racquet. But if you extend your racquet with the wrist already rotated, the racquet face will automatically contact the ball properly.

Also, if you don't rotate, you have a tendency to chop down on the ball, putting underspin on the hit. This causes two problems—the ball floats up to the front wall, and the reverse spin will pull the ball down to the floor, bringing it up higher into the opponent's power zone. The underspin gives the opponent more time to see and react to the shot and to retrieve it.

WHEN TO ROTATE

The rotation is simply an adjustment from the No. 2 position, or middle position, on the racquet, to the No. 1 position for a right-handed player or to the No. 3 position for a lefty. The rotation comes in between ready positions as you maneuver to the ball. It becomes an automatic thing, and the more you practice the little turn—it's only ¼ inch—the quicker you'll be able to do it.

THE BACKHAND GRIP

Grab the racquet with the palm flat in a trigger grip. Don't put your thumb on the side of the racquet, but rather keep it wrapped around the middle finger. If the thumb is up, you won't be able to turn the racquet as easily, thus losing power and eliminating the snapping of the wrist at

Backhand trigger grip.

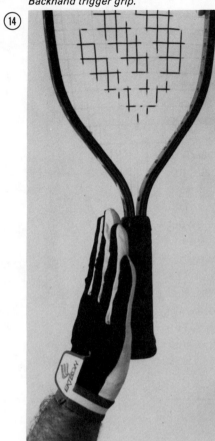

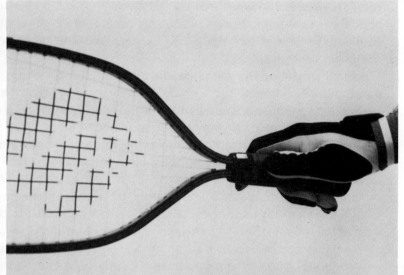

Incorrect thumb position for the backhand trigger grip.

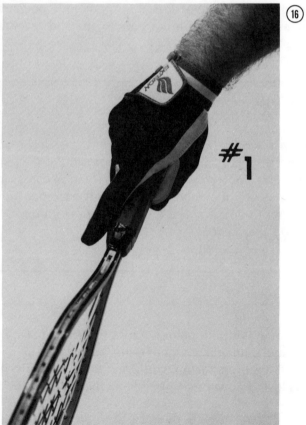

Correct thumb position for the backhand trigger grip.

the extension of your swing—the source of power in the stroke. Also the vibration of the racquet will not be transferred throughout your entire body; it will instead be isolated in the wrist and elbow and possibly the shoulder, putting strain on elbow and wrist. Over a period, this could cause injury that would end your racquetball-playing career.

THE BACKHAND READY POSITION

You should be facing the side wall, and as the ball approaches, your racquet should be drawn up to shoulder level as quickly as possible, elbow at the level of the base of your sternum, about 3 to 4 inches from your body. Now bring the racquet back to your opposite shoulder,

Side-wall stance with correct racquet positioning for the Backhand Ready Position.

staying at shoulder height, with the top of the racquet pointing to the ceiling. Don't rotate too far; it cuts reaction time and causes overspin on the ball. Rotate just enough so the racquet hand is even with the back shoulder.

At this point you should be able to draw a direct line from the opposite shoulder to the crease in your elbow. Important: You want to keep your racquet pointing to the ceiling, because if you don't you'll undercut the ball.

THE V POSITION

The V is simply the imaginary line drawn down the hand and forearm. If you look at it, you'll notice it forms a V. This may sound silly, but it's an extremely important part of the backhand. If you begin the stroke

incorrectly and have to adjust during the moment, you're inviting inconsistency. Which also invites disappointment.

Common Mistake: Don't move your arm up into the V. This just lengthens the swing (we don't need any excess motion when a ball is approaching at 90 mph) and forces you into a vertical stroke, swinging with the racquet head facing straight to the floor. A vertical stroke is nice if you hit the ball perfectly—off the front foot, say 6 inches above the floor—but what if your opponent angles the ball into your body? If you're late with your stroke and have to hit the ball behind your power zone, a vertical swing will send the ball up the wall in the first case and skip in the latter. If you're early, a vertical swing will cause the ball to rise up to the front wall, leaving an easy set-up for your opponent. That gives you only one chance in three to make the shot.

SHOT SEQUENCE FOR THE BACKHAND: As a result of moving your racquet back to the opposite shoulder, a V will form along an imaginary line drawn from your hand and forearm up to your shoulder (#18). Do not extend your shooting arm too far forward. This elongates the stroke and limits your shot capability. Instead keep the racquet back. Side view (#19) and front view (#20) are shown.

THE STEP

The step is the same as for the forehand: Feet shoulder width apart, front foot angled 45 degrees. The key here is how the elbow moves during the swing. It should be pushed out and around—like throwing a Frisbee straight ahead—with the elbow gradually extended in one smooth movement. If the elbow extends in two moves—out, then around—you'll quickly find yourself with elbow problems.

SHOT SEQUENCE CONTINUED: *Your footwork for the backhand is just like that for the forehand—front foot angled at 45 degrees. The swing then revolves around the elbow, which remains at sternum height, pushing out and around in one smooth movement (#21). When your elbow reaches the inner thigh of your front foot, your arm should gradually extend, with contact coming off the big toe of the front foot (#22). In the follow-through (#23), you want the racquet moving toward the front wall. The opposite arm should not hug the body or pull backward; rather it should just follow its natural course.*

At the start of the backhand (#24), you can grip the throat of the racquet with the index finger and thumb of the opposite hand—not with the hand itself.

CONTACT

Set up an imaginary wall at your inner thigh. When your elbow leads through and hits that point, your arm should gradually extend around. Again, these are not two separate motions, but rather two instruments played in concert. The elbow leads, the arm follows. And keep the elbow at sternum height. Keep your racquet up.

The contact comes at your extension point—front foot, big toe.

The purpose of the "out and around" motion is to make the racquet face come out and around, setting up square contact.

To hit the shot, don't change your stroke. *Don't move the body and angle of your shoulder.* Go down or up to get a shot. Don't move with your arm but with your body. The wrist snap is merely a product of the arm extension and the proper contact point.

FOLLOW-THROUGH

You want your racquet to end up going toward the front wall for three reasons: It keeps an even trajectory, the ball plays better off the strings, and it is safer. (It keeps the hitter from going around 270 degrees, which can make an impression on the face or dental work of an opponent.)

Let me relate a story about safety. In my very first tournament, I reached the men's B finals in El Paso, Texas, where I faced a guy named Jimmy Latham who could do it all—rollouts, behind-the-back shots, between-the-legs shots, everything. He crushed me 21-2 in the first game. Somehow I lucked out and won the second, 21-19, but I was losing 18-1 in the third when ol' Jimmy got a little too close to my backhand. I followed through behind my head and knocked Jimmy right in the forehead. He was out cold. I won the tournament, but it taught me—and Jimmy—a lesson we'll both never forget.

THE OPPOSITE ARM

Again, this thing acts like a younger brother on a hot date—you don't really want it around. I've found it handy to grip the throat of the racquet with the index finger and thumb of my opposite hand. *Don't grip with* the hand itself! It inhibits movement and slows down racquet speed. Don't grab the top, either; the tendency there is to pull down on the racquet, which unlocks the wrist. Also, don't hug yourself with the opposite arm to keep it out of the way. This inhibits shoulder rotation, decreasing power. And don't pull away backward. This is counterproductive, pulling against your natural forward momentum. And you'll look like you're taking a swan dive, and we're not diving here. Just let your arm follow its natural course. That should be in the same trajectory as your racquet arm.

CHECKLIST FOR THE BACKHAND

1. Rotate your grip ¼ inch to the left from the forehand as you maneuver to the ball.
2. Grip the racquet with the trigger grip, remembering to keep the thumb wrapped around the middle finger and not against the back of the racquet. Otherwise you'll lose potential power and possibly cause injury to arm, elbow, or shoulder.
3. Draw the racquet back at shoulder level, elbow at base of sternum, 3 to 4 inches from the body, until it reaches the back shoulder. Keep the top of the racquet pointing to the ceiling. Don't rotate too far—it cuts reaction time and forces overspin on the ball.
4. Set up for the shot just as for a forehand: feet a shoulder width apart, front foot at a 45-degree angle. Arm action starts with elbow leading, then extended at midthigh. The arm will follow out and around in one smooth movement, like throwing a Frisbee straight ahead. Contact the ball off the big toe of the front foot.
5. To hit different shots, move the body, not the racquet and arm. Wrist snaps automatically with arm extension.
6. Let your other arm follow the natural course of the racquet. Don't hug body or pull back.
7. For balance, hold the racquet throat with index finger and thumb. Nothing else.

5
FINE-TUNING THE
MIND AND BODY

*T*o be a winner, you have to learn to prepare yourself mentally and physically for an upcoming match. I find it most effective to do my stretching and thinking in a relaxed environment, a private place somewhere in the club where I can be by myself and not hear balls banging off the walls and players screaming. Of course, finding solitude in racquet clubs with as many as 4,000 members isn't easy, but there are better places to prepare for a match than in the cold, damp hallway outside a court.

For the physical warm-up, one of the best places to unwind is the whirlpool, if the club has one. I came to the conclusion long ago that I'm lazy when it comes to stretching, so I look for help. Use a whirlpool. Or for clubs without whirlpools, a sauna, or a Jacuzzi. Anywhere where it's warm so stretching muscles is easier. Warning: Don't stay in too long or you'll find yourself tired and lethargic. And as far as what exercises to do, any reputable club will have a stretching chart. Follow those closely and you'll be fine.

The second part of my warm-up, which goes hand in hand with the physical, is preparing my mind for the game. What is my purpose in this match? What will I be trying to accomplish? I ask myself these questions, forcing my mind to focus on the task ahead. What I've also found of great value is a concept called visualization. You visualize in your mind what you want to happen on the court, imprinting a mental image in your mind of the perfect backhand stroke, a crisp forehand, smooth movement to the ball, etc.

If you take the time to warm up your body, formulate a game plan, analyze your opponent's strengths and weaknesses, and then picture some perfect shots in your head, you'll find yourself points ahead of other players before the first serve is ever hit.

PRACTICE

One of the best things about racquetball is that you can practice alone; you don't need someone to pitch you a ball or catch your passes. You don't need to practice more than half an hour once or twice a week—that's more time than most C and B players devote—but when you do decide to practice, either alone or with a partner, you should take it seriously. What you're striving for are shots that don't break down when a match heats up.

To facilitate this, use your imagination. Devise drills that sharpen your body and mind. Some simple suggestions follow.

1. Have one person work on serving while the opponent returns. Switch when one tires of serving. You can prolong the rally one stroke by allowing the server to play the return and go for the pass or kill. You can even play out the rally if that's agreeable, but avoid keeping score; the theme here is working on the mechanical and seeing what the ball does in certain situations. Consider it a dress rehearsal, not the real thing.

2. Have your partner line up at the BW $1\frac{1}{2}$ and $3\frac{1}{2}$ locations and hit down-the-line shots and crosscourt passes. Your job is to play center court and attempt to cut off the passes, putting away winners of your own. Hit 20 pinches from each side and then switch.

3. Play a reaction game from the service-line area. Stand side by side with your partner and alternately hit shin-high shots into the front wall at each other. The object is to try to kill or pass each other without letting the ball touch the ground. This is great for developing hand-eye coordination and the reflexes you'll need to play front court.

4. Practice ceiling shots just as they would happen during a regular game.

5. If you get bored with the above, try something like a Lobster Ball Machine. This machine is excellent because it will force you to hit shots on the run and allow you to work on hard-to-simulate shots over and over again, thus improving performance.

A SPECIAL WORKOUT

Imagine the back of the court laid out in an X as shown in the diagram. The numbers define certain spots on the court. There's a definite reason for practicing in the back one-third of the court: Most racquetball games are won by shot-making in that area (a child could hit kill shots from the short line), so you want to be ready to play in the last 15 feet of the court, not the first 25.

When practicing, start slow at all the positions. Just try to get a feel for the shot, picking up the tempo accordingly. Position by position, here's a short "how to":

Position 1: Hit 60–65 shots, dropping the ball slowly into your power zone. The last 20–25 shots should be hit at near full speed.

Position 2: Hit pinch shots, to both sides, dropping ball into power zone. Hit about 30 to each side, last 10 or so at full tilt.

Position 3: Same as from position 1, just opposite stroke.

This X pattern marks the five best spots for serious practice and the standard prematch warm-up.

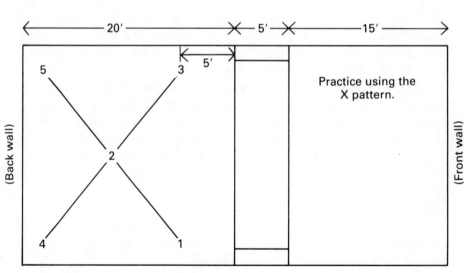

Position 4: Back-wall drills. Keep your shoulders square to the side wall. Bounce the ball off the floor so that it hits the back wall and drops into your power zone. Hit 30–35 down-the-line drives and crosscourts, 10 or so at full speed.

Position 5: Same routine as Position 4; use opposite stroke.

For a prematch warmup, just play the X game, again starting slow and increasing the pace. But hit only half as many shots as when practicing, as you'll only need ten or fifteen minutes, not thirty, to get warmed up.

CONDITIONING

I honestly believe conditioning is one of the most overlooked aspects of racquetball, and it shouldn't be, because all else being equal, as it is many times on the pro tour, the better-conditioned athlete will win. I can't tell you how many matches I've won because I've been in better shape.

My philosophy is that racquetball is both an aerobic and an anaerobic sport. By definition that means you derive both long-term and short-term cardiovascular benefits from playing, if you play hard. The aerobic benefit comes from playing at a vigorous pace for more than twenty minutes (usually in a pro match it's more like two hours). The anaerobic benefit is derived from the short, rapid bursts we take in chasing after the ball.

If you are an avid racquetball player—and by that I mean someone who plays more than once a week and likes to test himself in tournaments—it's important you make your workout and training *harder* than a tournament match can possibly be. You want tournaments to be the reward for all the work you've put in. You want to be prepared for anything. There's nothing more embarrassing than to have to call a time-out at 3-3 of the first game, or staring at the four walls knowing you can't go anywhere—your only choice is to open the court door and request another time-out.

With that in mind, I don't think you can overemphasize the relationship between weight training and racquetball. When all else is equal, the stronger opponent will win. Being physically fit also allows you to run longer and last longer on the court, and protects you from injury.

Upper body and leg conditioning are an important part of your game.

26 C

26 D

For the last eight years I've increased my strength by incorporating a series of standard Nautilus routines into my exercise. Three times a week I'll spend three to six hours on the machines, working my leg, arm, shoulder, and abdominal muscles. Any health-club instructor or Nautilus training center will be able to put together a sport-specific program to help you "muscle up." Also for your legs, you might want to consider using a stationary bike. I spend a great deal of time on a LifeCycle, a high-quality computerized training bike that simulates hill riding through a preset program. You don't need to get that sophisticated, but a few hours a week on a stationary bike certainly won't hurt your on-court performance. Racquetball is a game played with your legs, and when your legs go, so does your mind. You avoid taking that extra step that will make the ball fall in your power zone. Instead you hit the ball a little farther ahead and either miss high on the front wall or try to compensate with the racquet and end up skipping a shot into the floor. In racquetball, shortcuts eventually lead to dead ends.

ON-COURT CONDITIONING

It's probably more fun to make up your own drills, to let your imagination run wild, but here are a couple of on-court conditioning drills to help improve quickness and foot speed.

Drill No. 1: Put a glove down in the No. 2 position of the service zone. Start at back wall center and run and touch the glove. Run to the right side wall, then come back to the glove. Then front wall to glove. Then left side wall to glove. Remember to bend down and touch the glove with your hand every time. Do five sets of these glove drills at full blast.

Drill No. 2: Start at back wall center. Run to the short line and back. Then the service line and back. Then the front wall and back. Then the service line and back. Then short line and back. Repeat the drill three times without stopping.

6
THE SERVE

*T*he serve is probably the most important weapon in your game, but it's one of the misused and overlooked aspects of the sport. Serving is the only time during the match in which you have complete control of the situation. You are stationary, the ball is in your hand—it's important to take advantage of this. However, first you must ask yourself: What am I trying to accomplish with my serve? Too many racquetball players just rush right into their serves. They drop and hit the ball without purpose. Serving is an offensive weapon. It can win or lose a match, and if you don't know what you're trying to accomplish you might as well get into a car and go for a drive without any destination.

Serving is something of a chess match, so it's doubly important to experiment, at least at the outset of a game. Probe your opponent's game. Discover his or her weaknesses. Then exploit them. Find out what serves force your opponent into weak returns that permit you to put the ball away.

To start with, scout out your opponents. If you're playing a tournament, spend time checking out your division. Some players are afraid to watch future opponents. They feel this will actually psych them out. But it won't if you go into the scouting with a clear mind and a laundry list of what to look for. For example:

1. Does your opponent have problems with the drive serve?

2. Does he or she have a tendency to lean in one direction, anticipating a certain serve?

3. Does your opponent like the ball into the body, up, down?

4. Does he or she have a good ceiling game?

5. Is your opponent aggressive with the ball or does he or she prefer to play defense?

6. Does your opponent react to the shot down low or does he or she continually take it up high?

Once you discover an opponent's strengths—stay away from them. Conversely, there's always a weakness, a particularly vulnerable part of an opponent's game, and you owe it to yourself, once you find it, to take advantage of it. I realize that in most friendly "let's have a beer afterward" games it's difficult to watch a pal struggle with say, high lob serves to the backhand as you pound away point after point. You may want to let off the pressure, particularly if your opponent is buying dinner and you're famished! So hit a couple of serves to the forehand. Also, if you're scoring all your points off serve, you're losing the exercise and sweat factor of the sport. You decide. Sometimes a compromise works best. One of my workout partners is so susceptible to half-lob serves to backhand, I kill him every time I use that tactic. But what's it worth to me? Not much. So I hit the drive to his forehand, which he jumps on, clicking his entire game into gear. Of course, when it gets close, you know where my serve is going. . . .

SERVING AGAINST SOMEONE FOR THE FIRST TIME

Let's say you've had no time to scout out an opponent. The referee says, "Play ball," and it's your turn first. What do you do? Well, there's a rather systematic approach to getting to know your opponent on the run, so to speak.

Hit a drive serve to the backhand. If it gets killed, hit it again on your next serve. The first shot may have been a fluke. If your opponent rolls out the second time, it's obviously an indication he or she doesn't mind drive serves. So change it up: Kick in a half-lob, a Z, altering the speed and angle. Then watch the reaction. I remember playing pro Scott Hawkins in a tournament and discovering he hated, absolutely hated, a slow Z to the forehand. It took some time, but I found his weakness. So be patient. The worst thing you can do is say: "I'm gonna go hit that drive serve until hell freezes over." Well, hell won't freeze over—the game will be over. So think adjustment, making your opponent do what he or she doesn't want to do.

SERVICE MOTION FOR POWER SERVES

The forthcoming advice applies to the power drive and the power Z. (The Z is a serve which hits the front wall, then the side wall, before it bounces into the back court off the other side wall, parallel to the back wall.) It's important, given deception as the key to serving, that you *always serve with the same motion*. That's one of John McEnroe's biggest assets in tennis. Whether he's hitting a bullet down the service line or kicking a high shot to your backhand, his service motion never varies. You can't anticipate shots because the service motion itself varies only slightly—it is the ball that is dropped in different areas according to the serve.

WHERE AND HOW TO STAND

Your placement in the service zone will vary with the type of serve, but for the moment place yourself in the middle of the box, your right foot (if you're a righty) on the short line. The left foot should be 12 to 18 inches in front and your feet should be 4 to 5 inches apart. I prefer this wider base because it offers stability and balance, indispensable qualities if you want to keep control of the service situation.

Now lean back on the back foot. Slowly extend the racquet arm, bringing the opposite hand, which is holding the ball, into contact with the strings of your racquet. Drop your knees and slowly ease down, but not too far; one of the most common mistakes is to bend too far. This only serves to fatigue the legs in a long match and increases your range of motion, which invites mistakes. Keep it simple. Dip down 6 to 8 inches and don't bend at the waist, as this causes wasted motion and may result in a back injury.

THE SERVE: *Your stance will vary according to your serve—this is the drive serve.*

The front foot should be 12 to 18 inches in front, your feet 4-5 inches apart. Leaning on the back foot, slowly extend the racquet arm, bringing your opposite hand, the one holding the ball, into contact with the racquet.

Leaning on the back foot, slowly extend the racquet arm, bringing your opposite hand, the one holding the ball, into contact with the racquet.

Slowly ease down 6-8 inches, remembering not to bend at the knees.

SETTING UP THE SERVE: THE STEP AND DROP

Properly serving and deceiving your opponent comes from mastering and performing three separate functions almost simultaneously. Simply, it's *step, drop,* and *lift arm into the ready position.* This must be done in one fluid, never-changing motion. To begin, take a step back with your right leg even with the short line. How far back depends on the length of your legs. My brother Gregg has long legs and big feet, and he steps farther back than I do. But what's important is not to step back *too* far, leaving you off-balance as the serve motion begins.

Step-drop-serve.

32

Contact is made with forehand stroke off the inner thigh.

The hips then follow through, generating power.

(36)

(37)

Common Mistake: Don't twist your back leg around your front leg when stepping back. It limits the distance between you and the front line and rotates the hip toward the back right corner, turning your back to the front wall. This is excess motion, excess shoulder rotation, and your power is generated not from the shoulder rotation, but rather from the hips.

The drop aspect of the serve is often completely overlooked—and with disastrous results. As in the tennis "toss," the drop in racquetball, if executed properly, adds a consistency to your serve. You can't keep changing your drop location and expect to put the ball into tight spots.

So first, don't pull the ball away from the racquet; it's inefficient and inconsistent, and affords the returner an unnecessary look at the ball. Just drop the ball as if you're petting a dog on the head or the back. Your drop hand should move 4 to 6 inches forward. This adds overspin to the ball (you'll be "rolling over" the ball). As you step back you should prepare to put your hand into "petting" position. Now bring the racquet up and into the ready position as the ball is being dropped. When it is, use the forehand stroke. No salutes. No exaggerated shoulder rotation. Just a normal step so that as the ball drops into the power zone, the contact point will be the inner thigh, front foot angled at 45 degrees. The hips then shift through the swing, generating power.

The proper drop: Hold the ball with your thumb against the palm of your hand, applying spin as you drop.

As the ball drops, raise your racquet into the ready position.

SERVES—X DOESN'T MARK THE SPOT

In so many instruction books and in some courses offered by professional teachers, Xs are taped on walls and students are told to hit at this X for the Z serve, this X for the lob, this X for the power Z, and so on. The truth is that X doesn't mark the spot. It can't, because a short player has a different trajectory to that X than a tall player.

In the drive serve, for example, it's not how hard you hit the ball but *the angle* at which you contact the front wall. It's critical that the ball be *going up* to the front wall, not straight, or when it hits the wall it will level off, drop, and come up short.

THE ART OF SERVING:
Use the same forehand stroke, but contact the ball at different angles for different serves (#41). Remember to keep your shoulders on the same plane as the swing (#42,43,44).

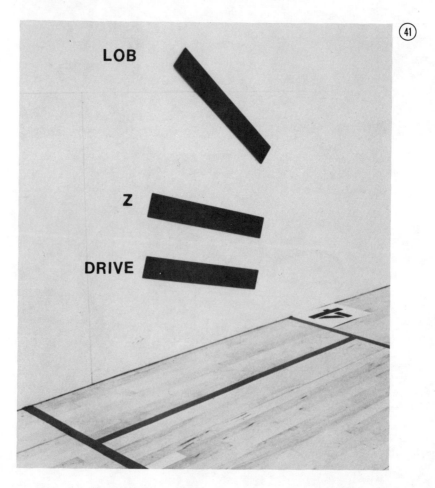

LOB

Z

DRIVE

41

(42)

(43)

(44)

In my clinics I illustrate this point with the Joe Wittenbrink story. Joe, a guy I play in El Paso, hits the drive serve harder than any pro, including Marty Hogan. We're talking about 3,000 mph here, or at least it seems that fast. One problem: Most of the time Joe comes up short. He's got no idea on angle; the ball is always coming straight into the wall and dropping off, despite the velocity. Sometimes it will bounce three times before it hits the back wall. I shouldn't say this about Joe, because I know that when he learns of the problem he'll probably beat the heck out of me.

Anyway, serving is very individualistic, but generally the contact point for a drive serve is between the shin level and the knee level, depending on the angle of the shoulder. But remember, you want to take the ball up at an angle where your *shoulders are on the same plane as your swing.* This means not bending down with your shoulder, leaning over into the shot, then trying to "scoop" the ball up from shin to knee. And don't isolate on racquet movement. The trajectory of the raccuet is based on the angle of your hips and shoulders. So get those shoulders and hips lined up at a spot on the front wall and you'll be in the driver's seat before you know it.

Z SERVE

Once more, X doesn't mark the spot. Contact point is generally at knee level to midthigh. The higher you travel up the leg, naturally, the higher on the wall the serve will go and the deeper it will move into the court. If hit at shin level a solid Z will land just beyond the service line, short and ripe for your opponent.

HALF-LOB

This is a defensive serve, a shot that just kisses the front wall softly— fairly high up—then drifts upward in an arc that takes it deep into the backcourt. The lob is the *exception* to the rule. Contact it (1) as it rises off the floor and (2) with a shorter stroke, actually more of a push.

And face it, you're not going to fake anyone out, so take an open stance with your legs apart. Invert the arm, bringing the elbow into the side (unlike a forehand stroke), lifting the arm up and pushing with the racquet. Contact is at waist level, angling up to the shoulder level. You're lifting the ball, remember, not hitting through it. By lifting you are increasing the arc to the front wall, which produces a higher bounce and tougher return, because the ball is dropping down at a sharper angle off the back wall; and putting topspin on the ball, which increases the arc even more.

SERVING BY THE NUMBERS

In my system of serving, which places a premium on deception and variety, you don't have to think where to hit the wall to hit, say, a low drive serve to the backhand. You play the numbers and serve from 3 on the service line (S 3) to 2 on the front wall (FW 2). You can use the zone as a landmark to guide shots consistently into the proper areas.

Drive Serve to Backhand, Righty Versus Righty

Setup is from S 3 to FW 2. Now, some may immediately say: Why S 3 and not S 2 to FW 2? Two reasons: There is not enough angle for the drive from S 2 to FW 1 to get the service into the critical backcourt area, a place where the game is won or lost strategy-wise; and it takes too much time and effort to get to center court from S 2.

The S 3 to FW 2 drive affords several advantages. The increased angle on the drive serve makes it easier to drive the ball into the 5-foot back-corner buffer zone, an area whose cramped dimensions make it difficult for you to get your body into the proper position to make consistent returns; your opponent can't see as easily where the ball is going because you're shielding the ball with your body; and the drop to the center zone is a quick, efficient shuffle.

Z Serve to Forehand, Righty Versus Righty

Keeping the ball within the power zone, step from S 3 to FW 2. This makes the opponent think it's another backhand drive. Remember, deception is the key, so don't telegraph tendencies. The stroke will remain the same but with two important differences:

1. Drop the ball about 2 inches in front of the power zone.

2. Bring your racquet "around" the ball in an arc which will take the ball to FW 1. The wrist snap at impact will be the same. You'll just be hitting the serve a little farther out in front and with a wider arc.

DRIVE SERVES: *The best place to hit the forehand drive serve to the backhand is S 3 to FW 2 (#45). On the Z drive serve, righty versus righty, it's best to play it S 3 to FW 1 (#46). This can be done by dropping the ball 2 inches in front of the power zone and bringing your racquet "around" the ball. Another solid serve from the S 3 position is the power drive—S 3 to FW 3½ (#47).*

By keeping the motion the same and changing the placement of the drop, you keep your opponent frozen, unable to cheat in any direction on your serve until it's too late.

Other Serves from S 3

Just because you're serving from here doesn't mean you have to limit yourself to the power drive to the backhand and the Z. You can always toss in the power drive to the forehand (S 3 to FW 3½). To do this, step in the same direction as for the drive to backhand and power Z (S 3 to FW 2). Otherwise you'll telegraph the serve. But instead of dropping the ball in the middle or out front of your power zone, let it fall a little behind the power zone. Then drive the shot to F 3½, remembering to contact the ball square with *full racquet extension*. If not, the ball will not go straight down the line but instead kick off the side wall into the middle.

Power Z to Backhand

On this serve, you want to alter your position. Some might say, from looking at "the numbers," that the best serving position would be S 2.

Wrong. From S 2 you cause yourself problems, mainly because the angle of the front wall/side wall shot brings it directly back at the server and there's a good chance of getting blown out of the middle because the ball will ricochet directly into center court. Also, it's difficult to angle the serve into the 5-foot buffer zone. Therefore, hit the Z from S 1, aiming for FW 3. This increases the angle of the shot, taking it deeper into the left backhand corner. It also increases the spin of the ball as it kicks off the left side wall, staying parallel to the back wall.

Alternative Serves from S 1

You can also hit to FW 2 for a drive forehand, hitting the ball behind the power zone.

Stroke S 1 to FW ½ for a backhand drive, hitting the ball a little more in front of the power zone and swinging around, as in the power Z to the forehand.

Half-Lob

S 3 to FW 2 brings the ball back left into the 5-foot buffer zone. Use S 3 rather than S 2 because the angle is better into the buffer zone.

POWER Z TO BACK-HAND: From an altered position (S 1 instead of S 2), aim for FW 3 (#48). This increases the angle of the shot, taking it deeper into the back left corner.

ALTERNATIVE SERVES FROM S 1: *Drive fore-hand to FW 2 (#49), accomplished by hitting the ball a bit behind the power zone. A backhand drive—S 1 to FW 1/2—is simply a matter of hitting the ball a little in front of the power zone (#50).*

Slow Z

S 3 to FW 1 for the forehand. S 1 to FW 3 for the backhand.

To keep the Z within the buffer zone, remember this little formula: EVERY FOOT FROM THE BUFFER ZONE MEANS AN ADDITIONAL 1 INCH TO THE RIGHT OR LEFT ON THE FRONT WALL, DEPENDING ON WHETHER THE BALL HITS OFF THE SIDE WALL (1 INCH TO THE RIGHT) OR BACK WALL (1 INCH TO THE LEFT). So, if your serve is 2 feet short on the side wall, you know you must adjust and move your serve 2 inches to the left on the front wall.

7
SERVICE RETURN

*O*ne of the building blocks of the game—and the easiest to master—is the service return, but unfortunately, for some reason instructors tend to make it the most complicated. They shouldn't.

You want to avoid confusion in service return. Racquetball is an action-reaction sport. If your mind is muddled as a shot approaches, you'll end up hitting weak, ineffective returns. Therefore, your return-of-serve philosophy should be a simple one: Play defense, make your opponents earn their points, take high-percentage shots, keep the server out of the critical center-court position, and set up scoring shots of your own.

Now this may seem complex for such an elemental aspect of the game, but it's not. All the above suggestions can be boiled down into one sentence: *Use standard shots for standard heights.* This means in certain areas of the court, when the ball is served into a particular area of your body, react with a specific shot into a specific area. Nothing more, nothing less. Just as you serve "by the numbers," you return the serve in the same way.

WHERE TO STAND AND HOW TO MOVE

Your positioning for return of serve is simple. The best spot is a racquet swing away from the back wall in the middle of the court. If you stand too close to the back wall, you'll be vulnerable to drive serves just past the short line. If you're too close to the server, power Zs and deep drive serves become a problem.

In moving to the serve, your first step—contrary to popular opinion—is *not* a crossover. On a shot to the left side wall, a move where your right leg crosses over your left just decreases mobility and stability. Your feet can get tangled up. Your first move should always be with the foot closest to the side wall toward which the ball is angling. For example, if the ball is served to the left, the left foot leads, and vice versa. This allows you to judge what the ball is doing and take stock of your return shot before actually hitting it.

Conversely, when moving to the ball you don't want to be thinking about what shot to hit—only *where* you're going to hit the right shot. Thinking what shot you're going to hit should be done before the serve is hit, not after.

SERVICE RETURN: The best spot to stand is a racquet swing away from the back wall in the middle of the court (#51).

(52)

GETTING READY: *From your basic service return stance (#52)—feet about shoulder width apart, racquet ready—your first step should always be with the foot closest to where the ball is heading (#53). Do not use a crossover step (#54).*

(53)

(54)

READING THE SERVER

Many people, particularly those playing regularly at the club or recreational level, do a lot of talking with their bodies. If you can learn to read this "body language," to look for little idiosyncrasies and tendencies, you can be in the right spot at the right time almost all the time.

If you have a chance, scout out your opponent before a match. Look for little giveaways, a regular rub of the nose before the drive serve to the forehand, scooting back a couple of feet in the service box before hitting a hard drive serve down the line, looking back to where the serve is supposed to end up before the ball is actually hit. Unless the server has adopted our service method (which places a premium on deception), chances are something will show up.

And once you know what is coming, or think you know, the rule is: *Anticipate, don't commit.* It's okay to lean a smidgen or two in one direction, or to be thinking about playing what you believe will be a power Z, but don't commit. If you do, you won't be able to recover and return the unexpected serve. Remember, a good server is always watching your body language too.

THE CONTROL ZONE

Very soon the phrase "control zone" will appear, and you need a definition. The control zone simply refers to an area 5 feet behind the short line that, in my mind, resembles an egg on its side. To be in control in this zone, you simply want to be close to any shot that your opponent can possibly hit. Unfortunately for some of my more dogmatic students, the control zone doesn't stay in one spot. Rather it "floats" in relation to the ball and your opponent. But basically, if you can stay in front of your opponent in the orbital area 5 feet behind the short line, you'll do just fine.

SERVICE RETURN BY THE NUMBERS—RETURNING SERVES AT CHEST HEIGHT OR ABOVE

Immediate reaction, either forehand or backhand: Take the ball to the ceiling with a ceiling shot.

If the serve, most likely a lob or lazy Z, comes into your backhand, take it back to the side in which your competition is weakest, most likely the backhand. That means back wall 1 (BW 1) to FW $\frac{1}{2}$.

If the soft serve comes into your forehand, take the shot crosscourt to the ceiling, using FW 2 as your aiming point.

It's a mistake to deviate from this philosophy. Hitting down on the ball—an overhead kill or pass—is very difficult and is usually reserved for those with a high skill level. All you want to do in this situation is force your opponent from the center-court control zone and into deep backcourt.

Chest or above goes back to the ceiling (BW1-FW1/2).

RETURNING SERVES FROM WAIST TO MIDCHEST LEVEL

One option is to take the ball back to the ceiling.

Another option is to go with a high-percentage offensive shot, dictated by your opponent's position on the court and where the serve is headed.

In the latter case, think in terms of percentages. You have two suboptions: down the line or crosscourt. Both are one-wall shots. At this point, with the ball still above the waist, do not attempt a two-wall shot such as a side wall/front wall pinch. If you miss, the ball will almost certainly carom out into the control zone, which at the moment your opponent owns.

Mid-chest or below increases the options: you can either go back to the ceiling, or, more often, down the line or crosscourt.

56

Down the Line: For a righty with the ball at his forehand, hitting from BW 3-4, go to FW 3½-4. For a backhand, hit BW 0-1, aim for FW 0-½. For a southpaw, it's just the opposite.

Crosscourt: Both righties and lefties should shoot for FW 2.

Another advantage with these high-percentage shots is that even if you should miss, the ball will carom to the backcourt and force your opponent to hit a shot 38 to 39 feet from the front wall. It also pulls the opponent out of the control zone.

RETURNING SERVES FROM WAIST TO KNEE LEVEL

This is still a little high to think in anything other than percentage shots—and that means one-wall returns. Of course, it's important to note that in amateur and pro racquetball 60 percent of the shots travel crosscourt (it seems many people have a phobia about hitting down the lines; this is probably due to fear of the side wall), so most people gear into stopping crosscourt shots, moving back and away from your forehand. So mix it up. Your No. 1 percentage shot in this situation (as it could be in the waist to midchest shots) is down the line. Later, you can kick in a crosscourt for variety.

SERVICE RETURN AT KNEE HEIGHT OR LOWER

The ball is finally down where we want it. You don't have to swing down to kill it. If anything you want to miss on the upswing, because if you leave it up, you've still got a midcourt pass and the ball headed 39 feet away.

Option No. 1: Down the line. For a backhand to a righty, contact the ball at BW ½-1 and hit to FW ½. The ball should travel straight down the line. For a forehand, it's BW 3½-4 to FW 3½-4. Just switch the strokes around if you're a lefty.

Option No. 2: Crosscourt, BW 1 to FW 2.

SPECIAL SITUATIONS—TWO-WALL RETURNS

At the most basic levels, you want to stay away from two-wall returns until you've mastered one-wall play. But there are times when using two walls is advisable. For example, if your opponent is playing deep in the court, or leans a lot on his heels, waiting for kills and passes, that's when you would mix in a side wall/front wall pinch.

To hit a pinch shot, very little changes in your stroke mechanics. Only your body and ball position change. You want your front shoulder to move toward the proper corner (stepping in that direction with your

When your opponent plays deep in the back-court or leans on his heels it's okay to use two-wall returns.

front foot will do the trick), and you want to contact the ball slightly back in the power zone. This will cause the ball to travel to the side at which you are aiming. Aim for the small area within 1 foot from the front corner. You can pinch the ball in either way (hitting either front wall or side wall first) and be effective, but the ball stays closer to the front wall if you hit the side wall first.

Concentrate on that 1-foot-away area. The farther you move away from the corners, the greater the angle and the farther the ball will come back into the control zone.

ADJUSTING TO THE GREAT SERVES

It happens at least once every match. Someone blasts a drive serve to either side or unleashes a tremendous power Z. From a spectator's standpoint it looks hopeless. But there's hope, if you'll just remember that in this case all you're trying to do is neutralize a sorry situation, to keep a point alive.

Let's take the drive serve first. First and foremost, get your racquet to the ball. Nothing else matters. And when your racquet does make contact with the ball, you want the face to be pointing up, so if all you can do is just let the shot ricochet off the face, at least it will be headed high on the front wall. This will force your opponent deep into the backcourt, buying time for you to recover.

A LAST RESORT: When all else fails and you must take a serve off the back wall, the rule is that, it's not how hard you hit the ball but the angle at which you hit it. The key is keeping your racquet at a 45-degree angle (#59).

If you have the chance, try to "chop" at the ball, using wrist action. This puts underspin on the return, giving even greater height on the shot when it rebounds from the ceiling to the front wall to the floor, and making the ball travel deep into backcourt.

The power Z is something else. A perfectly hit Z will eventually carom off the side wall and run parallel to the back wall, sometimes as close as 12 inches from the back wall. In this case you have to try to get your racquet behind the ball and "flip" it up to the front wall, using just your wrist. Your destination point is the front wall, about 5 feet off the ground. If the shot hits much higher, chances are it will travel and rebound off the back wall, setting your foe up for an easy crosscourt or down-the-line winner.

LAST RESORT—HITTING OFF THE BACK WALL

This is a desperation shot only. If you're going to attempt it, remember *it's not how hard you hit the ball off the back wall, but the angle at which you hit it.* I can't tell you how many people I've seen slam shots into the back wall only to see the ball travel on a straight line up to the front wall, chest high, to be killed. Or worse, how many players have been hit in the head or eye by balls ricocheting from the back wall.

The key here is angle. You want to keep your racquet at about 45 degrees so that when the ball hits the back wall it comes out at the same angle it entered—on the rise. This will carry the shot up to the front wall, resulting in a high first bounce and a deep carry into the backcourt.

8
SITUATIONAL
RACQUETBALL

Shot selection on the racquetball court can be viewed much like a game of chess—knowing when and where to make your move, patiently setting up your opponent for a winner. But in the board game, the pieces move only in certain directions; in racquetball, plays aren't quite as predictable. So while our "by the numbers" system still works, one must understand that a spatial relationship exists on the court; you're not always going to be in the right spot to hit, say, a passing shot from BW 1 to FW 2. But if you know how to play the angles and have proper positioning, you'll see how little adjustments in shot location produce consistent results. The secret is, much as in chess, to know where your opponent is at all times, and what your options are. Can I pass him down the line? Should I go to the ceiling? What about crosscourt? In my system, you'll see that I rank percentage shots in order and offer variables so that when your opponent wises up to a certain situation and begins to rush forward, or to anticipate in a certain direction, you can alter your style of play.

Now, you may think that because racquetball is such a fast-moving game, millions of on-court situations exist. That's not really true, as I discovered a long time ago when I was teaching at a club in El Paso. A woman came up to me and asked for a lesson on shot selection. Well, to be honest, at that time I had no idea about what shots to hit in certain spots on the court; I hadn't really thought about it. Today I still believe most people play racquetball haphazardly, without a game plan to score points. But on that day in El Paso I watched players play all afternoon, eventually seeing how certain situations occur all the time on the court. It became obvious over the years that if players could recognize these situations, understand what percentage shots were available, then execute them, their games would dramatically improve.

I should know. Once I mastered "situational racquetball," it took me from a low open player to a professional in three years. Rallies became shorter. Unlike other people, I didn't let the ball bounce around, as it would on a roulette wheel. When my number came up, I took my shot. *Every shot had a purpose.* Some rallies took only one shot. Others took two or three. Sure, as I progressed and the competition became quicker and more experienced, it was tougher and tougher to knock opponents out early, but no more did I have that "flail away" mentality common to so many players. I was selectively placing the ball around the court, moving my opponent away from the control zone whenever possible and scoring more points than I ever had.

Situational racquetball can be broken down into six simple circumstances. They are:

1. Backhand set-up shot with opponent on a diagonal behind you. The opponent can be either in center court or deep backcourt.

2. Forehand set-up in center court with opponent off deep to your forehand.

3. In the No. 3 position on the court at the 5-foot line, opponent angled off behind you.

4. A backhand shot in the middle of the court, opponent off to your left and behind you.

5. Deep backcourt with opponent parallel to you.

6. Ball coming off back wall or in deep backcourt with opponent behind you in deep backcourt.

I'll analyze each of these situations separately in a second, but first some common rules:

Rule 1: The more walls involved in a shot, the harder it is to execute. So the deeper you are in the court, the more you should consider one-wall options for scoring.

Rule 2: Hit the ball back behind you when your opponent is on an angle behind you.

Rule 3: When you use pinch shots, particularly from the backcourt, always pinch to the side your opponent is located on because the ball will eventually carom away from him or her.

Rule 4: Keep all shot selections away from center court, because, more than likely, that's where your opponent is.

Rule 5: If you can take the forehand shot, take it, even if it means hitting from the opposite side of center court. Forehands are just surer shots for most people—they are more confident and comfortable with them—so you might as well take advantage of this fact instead of fighting it.

Situation No. 1—Backhand Setup With Opponent on Diagonal Behind You

The No. 1 percentage shot is FW ½ to BW 0. Why? It puts the ball deep into the backcourt, it's a one-wall shot, and after the shot you are near

SITUATION NO. 1: THE BACKHAND SET-UP WITH OPPONENT ON A DIAGONAL BEHIND YOU. The No. 1 percentage shot is FW ½ to BW 0 (#60A). It's efficient (one wall instead of two) and it puts the ball in the deep backcourt. The No. 2 shot is the sidewall/front wall pinch (#60B).

60 A

the control zone. Also, as you move into the control-zone position, backing up slightly into the center-court area, you're physically blocking your opponent's vision of the ball, as well as creating a presence, i.e., an intimidation factor. And if your opponent does retrieve the shot, it's 38 to 39 feet from the front wall, making it harder to execute a return.

The No. 2 percentage shot, particularly if the opponent is in back-court, is the side wall/front wall pinch. Just aim for the corner, making sure if you miss it's to the side-wall side. Hitting the side wall first slows down your shot; the front-wall carom forces the opponent to move into front court, making a passing shot that much easier.

Variables: Opponent charging the front wall, either trying to come around you, to your backhand side, or straight up the middle.
  No. 1 percentage: Down the line.
  No. 2 percentage: Crosscourt pass, BW 1 to FW 2.
  Both make it difficult for the foe to adjust on the run.

Situation No. 2—Forehand Setup in Center Court With Opponent Deep to Forehand

No. 1 percentage shot: Hit the ball behind you, using one wall. Hit FW about 1½ feet up (shin height). If you hit a kill in this situation, great—but it's not necessary. All you're trying to do is win a point.

No. 2 percentage shot: Pinch shot to side opponent is located on.

Variables: If your opponent is trying to get around you to the side, make it as simple as possible for yourself. Hit the ball down the line, along the forehand side.

SITUATION NO. 2: FOREHAND SETUP IN CENTER COURT WITH OPPONENT DEEP TO FOREHAND. The No. 1 shot here is to blast the ball behind you, using one wall, aiming at FW 1½ (#61A). The No. 2 shot is to pinch the ball to the side your opponent is on (#61B).

61 A

*If your opponent is
trying to get around you,
keep it simple and go
down the line to the
forehand side.*

Situation No. 3—In No. 3 Position on Court at About 5-Foot Line, Opponent Angled Off Behind You

No. 1 percentage: Down the line. Same reasons as stated in Situation No. 1.

No. 2 percentage: Pinch to right front corner.

No. 3 percentage: Pass down the left-hand side if opponent runs up.

SITUATION NO. 3: IN CENTER COURT AT ABOUT THE 5-FOOT LINE, OPPONENT ANGLED OFF BEHIND YOU. The highest percentage shots are, in order, down the line to FW 3 (#62A), a right-corner pinch (#62B), and a pass down the line to the left (#62C) if your opponent tries to run up to pick off a pass.

(62) A

62 B

62 C

Situation No. 4—Backhand in Middle of Court, Opponent Off to Backhand Behind You

No. 1 percentage: Pass to FW 3 position back behind you.

No. 2 percentage: FW pinch to side where opponent is, moving ball away from opponent along the front wall.

Variable: If your opponent sneaks in or goes around to your forehand side, blast the ball down the line. Your opponent will be on the run, making shot adjustments difficult.

SITUATION NO. 4: BACKHAND SHOT IN MIDDLE OF COURT, OPPONENT OFF TO BACKHAND BEHIND YOU. The No. 1 shot here is the pass—to FW 3 behind you. No. 2 is the FW pinch to the side of your opponent (#63B). If your opponent tries to sneak up and go around you to the forehand side (#63C), reply with a blast down the line.

63 A

63 B

63 C

Situation No. 5—Deep Forehand Shot With Opponent Parallel to You

No. 1 percentage: Hit the ball behind you, FW 1 to BW ½.

No. 2 percentage: Resist the urge to use a regular pinch to right front corner. If you miss, the ball will carom off the front wall, eventually trapping you against the left side wall, leaving the court wide open to your opponent. Instead, use a side wall/front wall pinch to the left corner. This is an alternative shot, one used when your opponent is getting familiar with your hitting the ball behind you. Or maybe he is anticipating, maybe even leaning a little too much to the side wall. So, when you hit the reverse pinch, the ball will actually move away from the opponent, "wrong-footing" the opponent, as we say in the game. But remember, this shot is based on position. If your opponent can't anticipate or react to the down-the-line pass, keep hitting it.

SITUATION NO. 5: DEEP FOREHAND SHOT WITH OPPONENT PARALLEL TO YOU. *Your best shot here is to hit the ball behind you, in this case FW 1 to BW 1/2 (#64A). If you think your opponent is expecting this shot, try a pinch shot, but resist the urge to pinch into the inviting right corner; instead hit a side wall/ front wall pinch to the near side (#64B).*

(64) A

(64) B

Situation No. 6: Ball Coming Off Back Wall or in Deep Backcourt With Opponent Behind You

No. 1 percentage: Crosscourt shot (FW 2½ to BW 4) behind you. Not a kill shot; just at shin height.

No. 2 percentage: Pinch shot to the side your opponent is on, the bounce off the front wall taking the ball away from the opponent.

Important: As you move along the back wall, it really doesn't matter too much where you are situated; you can respond with the same shots (behind you or pinch to the opponent's side) as long as the distance between you and your opponent stays the same. But if what was once the near corner slowly becomes the far corner of the court, you may want to replace the pinch to opponent's side with a side wall/front wall shot into the other corner.

65 A

65 B

**SITUATION NO. 6: BALL
COMING OFF BACK
WALL OR IN DEEP
BACKCOURT WITH
OPPONENT BEHIND
YOU.** *Your best bet
(#65A) is FW 2¹/2 to BW
4—hitting behind you,
not a kill, but just a shin-
high shot. Next, think
about a pinch (#65B) to
the side your opponent
is playing.*

9

POSITIONING AND

SOME SPECIAL SHOTS

*T*his part of the book could be subtitled "Being in the Right Place at the Right Time." One of the most difficult and frustrating adjustments for a novice player is learning to control his or her body, slowing it down or speeding it up, in relation to the speed and direction of the ball. It's not easy. One of the first instincts you have to overcome is chasing the ball, running around like a kid at recess as the ball whizzes from one side of the court to the other. This is a sport set in geometry; all roads (or angles, in this case) lead to center court or the control zone. You'd be wise not to stray too far from this spot, though you'll have to make adjustments when needed—adjustments we'll get to in a moment.

A second, more important point about positioning is safety. I believe one of the main reasons racquetball hasn't grown at an even faster rate is that many first-time or second-time players get out of position on the court, get hit with a ball or racquet, and never attempt to play again. If this is what the game is all about, they say, then the heck with it. But that doesn't have to happen. Most often these injuries are caused because people make one of two errors: Either they never move the head around to chart the flight of the opponent's shots, or they turn it *all the way* around. Either way they end up getting hit by a racquet or ball.

My feeling is that by turning your body a bit and using your peripheral vision you can see all you need to see on the court. I explain the how-tos in greater detail in the chapter on back-wall play, but suffice it to say here, you should never back straight up with your shoulders facing the front wall to play shots off the back wall. Instead you should turn to the side of the upcoming shot (forehand or backhand) and shuffle back, not crossing your feet. By using this method you can sight the ball out of the corner of your eye. And if you're leery of even this move, by all means wear eye protection (it should be mandatory for amateur play anyway). Protective eyewear will help decrease eye and face injuries, accidents that seem to occur more often in the novice and low intermediate divisions, because players in those classes are still learning when to look for the ball and are slow to recognize potentially dangerous situations.

What do you look for when you glance around? With a fast glance you should be able to decipher the direction of the shot. The key is watching your opponent's front shoulder.

One of the most common mistakes made in our sport is losing track of opponent and ball. You should use your peripheral vision or turn your body a bit to pick up the player and ball.

66

1. If it's pointing up, the ball is headed for the ceiling.

2. If it's square, the shot will be down the line.

3. If it's tucked in with front foot at a 45-degree angle, the shot will be a pinch.

If your opponent's front shoulder is pointing up, the ball is headed for the ceiling.

Tucked in, look for a pinch.

4. If it's open, the shot will be crosscourt.

Now these are not absolute, so consider it best to anticipate, *not* commit. The reason is simple. If your opponent mishits a shot, you're out of position and out of luck.

 B

If it's square, the ball will travel down the line.

 D

An open front shoulder means the ball will travel crosscourt.

HOW TO BE IN PROPER POSITION

What I have to say may seem too simple for all the complex situations a player faces on the court, but try it. The rule is this: *Imagine a diagonal line from where the ball is to the opposite corner. Place the balls of your feet on that imaginary line about 5 to 10 feet away from the shooter.*

LINING UP IN THE PROPER POSITION: To keep the correct spatial relationship between yourself and your opponent and the ball remember this simple rule: Imagine a diagonal line from where the ball is to the opposite corner. Place the balls of your feet on that imaginary line about 5-10 feet from the shooter. *Notice how this relationship never varies as the players move around the court.*

68 A

68 C

There are a couple of exceptions (which I'll get to in a second), but for the most part, it's that simple. Just use the ball, not your opponent, as your guide, and whenever possible match yourself up to that diagonal line. The beauty of this concept is that it allows you a clear view of both the ball and your opponent. It also allows you to use your peripheral vision (you can see the shooter out of the corner of your eye). Plus it gives him or her ample opportunity to hit the shot, avoiding those costly hinder calls.

(68) B

(68) D

This rule is extremely effective if used in the back two-thirds of the court, particularly for shots along the side walls or in the corners. Your positioning in this case should be about 5 feet up the diagonal line but not so far forward as to be near the short line. This would allow your opponent a decidedly easier scoring shot on his two available options—the pass instead of the kill.

The only exceptions to this diagonal rule are these:

1. When the ball is coming off the back wall and both players are in the midcourt area. In this case, simply align yourself to the opposite side of the stroke your opponent is hitting. Stay up at the 5-foot slash marks.

2. When play is in the control zone. Simply bisect the court vertically and stay right behind your opponent, keeping a distance of about 3 or 4 feet. You're accessible to any shot and not prone to hinder calls.

3. In the midcourt area from the control zone to the back wall, commonly called the "intermediate zone." Don't play behind your opponent if possible. Try instead to come around behind the opponent on the side opposite the opponent's racquet. One of my favorite—and rather sneaky—moves is to come around the non-racquet side, move up, then softly tiptoe back. Your opponent, seeing your shadow, will change from his original thought of a crosscourt pass to a down-the-line pass. If he or she does, you'll be back into position with the ball on your forehand side, to either take the ball back down the line with a drive pass or slam a shot back crosscourt yourself.

PLAYING UP CLOSE

It never fails. A couple of times a game you'll find yourself in the front quarter of the court, either playing a long rebound off the back wall or reacting to a fierce volley. The worst thing you can do in this situation—your opponent out of position or with a wide-open alley to shoot for—is get too fine, trying to finesse a shot that doesn't need finessing. The standard rule for playing up close is *hit the ball to the side your opponent is not on, using one wall.* How high? It depends on where the opposing player is located. If the opponent is in your shadow, you have to shoot lower, for a kill. If the opponent is in another time zone, just make sure you don't skip the shot.

Another important point is to know your opponent's strengths. For example, Mike Yellen, one of the top pro players, is very quick laterally, but slower moving forward and back. So with Mike I try to hit the lines and use more pinches. But if an opponent is slow laterally and quick front to back, I try to force lateral moves and thus keep the opponent off balance.

CEILING SHOTS

Ceiling shots are regarded as the court of last resort in racquetball. For the most part, your shot selection should be aggressive, but when you have to play defense, or feel you have to set up other shots against tougher competition, then go to the ceiling.

You normally hit this shot from deep in the backcourt, aiming for the ceiling about 3 feet from the front wall. The ball will then carom into the front wall, take its first bounce around the service zone, and rebound very close to the back wall. This forces your opponent out of the control zone and makes him or her deal with a high-bouncing ball that can be difficult to return.

It's important to try to direct your ceiling shots to your opponent's backhand corner, because this is usually a player's weakest link. If you can, you should try to keep the ball as close to the side wall as possible, so your opponent will have to scrape the wall to return the shot. If you miss, however, the ball will rebound out for a "plum" shot, so until you've mastered the shot in practice, aim for the safety of the middle of the court.

Ceiling rallies are often some of the longest and most boring in the sport, mainly because if one player hits a good ceiling shot, there is little the other player can do except go back to the ceiling. The break generally comes when one or the other player hits a weak ceiling shot. This may be a ball that mistakenly hits the front wall instead of the ceiling, bouncing off the back wall and into the front court for a setup, but most often the ceiling shot will come up short, allowing you better positioning to execute a pass, a down-the-line shot, or a kill shot. Remember, however, during good ceiling rallies you should always *stay back with* your opponent after hitting a solid ceiling shot. There's no reason to move forward and backward like a yo-yo.

Hitting the Forehand Ceiling Shot

This is basically a directional shot with a limited force. Simulate a sidearm throwing motion, angling your shoulders up toward the ceiling, remembering not to get too close to the ball. Make sure upon extension you're stretching to hit the ball. This facilitates natural pronation and extension of the arm. *Important:* Hit the ball within your power zone; the contact point will be at shoulder level.

69 A

69 B

FOREHAND CEILING SHOT: *Simulate a sidearm throwing motion (#69A and B), then extend the racquet, hitting the ball at shoulder level out in front of your body (#69C). Follow through up to the opposite corner (#69D).*

69 C

69 D

Hitting the Backhand Ceiling Shot

The mechanics here are the same—not too close to the ball, arm extension, hitting the ball out front, off the front toe. The mechanics are the same as the forehand: Point your shoulder angle up to the ceiling. *All you're doing is bringing your power zone up to your height.* The principles of a solid backhand don't change. All you're doing is bringing the power zone up to shoulder level.

(70) A   (70) B

BACKHAND CEILING SHOT: *Extend your arm to your back shoulder (#70A), allowing your elbow, just as in the ordinary backhand stroke, to lead into the shot (#70B). Follow through naturally (#70C).* Important: *The mechanics of this shot don't differ from those of the backhand stroke; you're just moving the power zone up to shoulder level.*

70 c

THE OVERHEAD

There are two types of overhead shots: the overhead drive and the overhead kill. The kill is a very risky shot that should be used only in special situations, while the drive is primarily a change-of-pace shot, a hybrid ceiling shot. I'm including the overhead in this book and not around-the-world shots (the so-called AWBs) because I feel AWBs are not for beginners or low intermediate players. A good ceiling shot will serve the same purpose as an AWB any time.

On the overhead, the mechanics for either shot don't differ. An overhead is hit only when the ball is *above* your head. To begin, rotate your shoulders so they're square to the side wall. Bring your opposite

71 A

71 B

arm up and point to the ball. Now bring your racquet back as you would to scratch your back. Your weight should be on the back foot as the racquet pulls back. Contact point is at front foot. As you hit the ball, step forward, bringing your opposite arm down to the floor. It's vital that the ball be contacted at the front foot; this allows natural arm extension and wrist snap to occur. Extend the racquet over the ball, aiming on the overhead drive for knee level on the front wall. This shot is not meant to be a winner, just a means of forcing your opponent to hit up on the ball,

THE OVERHEAD DRIVE: *Rotating your shoulders square to the side wall, bring your opposite arm up and point to the ball (#71A). Bring your racquet back as if to scratch your back (#71B), your weight planted on your back foot. Contact the ball off your front foot as you step forward (#71C). Extend the racquet over the ball, following through naturally (#71D).*

(71)c

(71)D

making a weak return. The three best places to hit the overhead drive are (1) down the side wall, forcing the opponent out of center court; (2) so it takes a bounce near the service zone and bounces into opponent's body; and (3) crosscourt again forcing the opponent out of center court.

Caution: Make sure you don't hit the shot too hard; it defeats the purpose by coming off the back wall, all set up.

The overhead kill is a shot to hit when your opponent is playing deep, leaning back on his or her heels, or looking up, expecting another in a series of ceiling shots. But beware—this is a very difficult shot to execute. If you hit the ball too low, or too far in front of your body, or too far back in the power zone (no snap or arm extension), 90 percent of the time it will hit off the front wall, bounce, and carom off the back wall for an easy set-up. So hit the shot well, aiming for the corners, and use it wisely.

10
PLAYING THE SIDE
AND BACK WALLS

*T*hose who are new to racquetball but have some athletic ability and a cursory knowledge of center-court strategy often feel pretty good prior to their first real match. But when the ball starts bouncing off the side walls, caroming out of corners, taking fiendish bounces off the back wall, they realize they still have something to learn about this game. I hope that after reading this chapter, you'll know the fundamentals and feel better when the ball starts bouncing.

PLAYING THE SIDE WALLS

It's important here to remember how the ball bounces off the walls and not to get too close to the walls. Let the ball rebound off to you. If you overreact or get too close to the wall, a slight unexpected bounce off a side wall could send the ball back toward the middle. So don't get too close. The ball may jam against your body, forcing you to make a weak, jabbing stroke.

To minimize your mistakes, try to move quickly into position on the edge of the control zone—a safe 3 to 4 feet from the wall, far enough away to swing without obstruction when the ball rebounds. Keep your racquet in its ready position, then react to the ball when it comes off the wall.

Your body should be in the basic forehand or backhand hitting position—front foot angled at 45 degrees—so that you can use your hips and shoulders when you take your swing. Don't lean over or anticipate certain types of shots. If the ball hits a crack, or somehow bounces off funny, you'll be out of position to hit your shot.

If the ball is hit in such a way as to hug the wall, you have no recourse; just hit your shot as smoothly and confidently as if the ball were in center court. All you can do is try to scrape the wall and hope for the best.

BACK-WALL PLAY

From beginner on up, back-wall play is one of the most difficult areas of the game to learn, but yet it is not an overwhelming aspect of the sport if some basic rules are followed.

They are: *Move your feet. Play the wall—don't let the wall play you. Stay on the balls of your feet, not your heels. Know the standard starting positions and what shots relate to each position.*

We'll get to just what standard starting positions are in a second, but first understand that there are three basic back-wall shots, all easily defined by the distance the ball rebounds off the back wall. Shot No. 1 is the ceiling ball coming off the back wall. This is by far the most difficult and frustrating shot to master. The ball is dropping at a sharp angle, so it's tough to get your racquet behind the ball—a very important part of back-wall play. Shot No. 2 is the ball that hits the front wall, bounces out into midcourt or so, then hits the back wall and bounces out into intermediate or control zone. Shot No. 3, called the BB back wall (for reasons I'm at a loss to explain), hits off the front wall and travels in the air on the fly to the back wall, then bounces out strongly to center court or beyond. It's the easiest back-wall shot to play.

In all three of these shots it's important to remember to *make sure your racquet is behind the ball square with the racquet head.* What you're striving for is racquet balance, so that if a shot happens to drop too deep in your power zone, you're not swinging down on the ball (which invites skips), but rather getting that arm around the ball and lining up square. This can be done if you use a sidearm motion similar to that of a pitcher in baseball.

Getting to the Ball

No matter where or how the ball is hit, you have to get off your duff, *move, move, move!* The most common mistake in back-wall play—the one that sets off a series of other miscues—is not setting up properly to hit the shot. Your first move as you follow the flight of the shot is *not to back up with your shoulders facing the front wall,* then turning (which takes your eyes off the ball) to see where the shot will hit. Not only does this method limit mobility (your feet often get tangled up looking this way and that) but it adds excess motion to your swing. This reduces the time you have to effectively hit a shot.

So instead of backing up, learn to quickly recognize the ball is bound for the back wall, then once you decide that it will rebound off the back wall, decide whether it's a forehand or backhand play. Then turn to the appropriate side and shuffle back with shoulders square to the side wall. Do not cross your feet on the shuffle, just use your peripheral vision, sight the ball across your body, and pick out the spot where you estimate it will hit. When you do get into your ready position, you'll be standing in one of my standard starting positions, or SSPs.

And just what are these SSPs? There are only three, and they all relate to the severity of the bounce off the back wall.

SSP No. 1: For ceiling shots that drop near the back wall. Set yourself up 2-3 feet from the wall.

SSP No. 2: When the ball bounces off the front wall, hits the back wall, and bounces out near the intermediate or control zone. Here your distance is 4 to 6 feet from the back wall.

SSP No. 3: The ball bounces off the front wall, hits the back wall, then bounces rapidly toward the service zone and front wall. Move quickly and position yourself anywhere from 8 to 12 feet from the back wall.

The mechanics of all three SSPs are simple. In the ceiling shot the No. 1 concern should be: "Do I take this ball off the wall or go back up to the ceiling?" The rule of thumb here is: *If the ball is dropping down toward your shoulders, take it back up. If the ball is traveling across your shoulder, play it off the back wall.*

(72)   (73)

Avoid a common mistake in ceiling shots off the back wall: Do not turn and face the wall, attempting to "scoop" the shot. By turning your shoulder you limit your power. Instead, square those shoulders to the side wall, and as the ball is in the air, get your racquet up into ready position. Your body position should be such that the theoretical "first bounce" off the back wall will land at your front foot. And if you miscalculate, *don't* try to adjust your swing—move your feet, shuffling forward or back to get into the proper position.

(74)

SHOTS FROM THE STANDARD STARTING POSITIONS: *If a ball is dropping down toward your shoulders (#72), take it back up to the ceiling. If the ball is moving across your shoulders (#73), play it off the back wall. On ceiling shots, resist the urge to turn and play the shot off the back wall. Instead, square the shoulders to the side wall and as the ball is in the air, get your racquet into the ready position (#74). Your body position should be such that the first bounce will be at your front foot.*

The positioning of the body on the other two SSPs is in the court area only. You still want to use the same mechanics, the same foot movement, the ball dropping into your power zone. Remember: If you miscalculate, make sure it's to the back court and not forward. It's much easier to shuffle forward to hit a shot than to move back, stop, and then set up.

SHOT SELECTION FROM THE STANDARD STARTING POSITIONS

Now that we've learned just what the SSPs are, we'll go one step beyond and tell you what shots to hit in each of those three positions. You'll find the shot selection very limited, and with good reason—the object in our sport is to score points or regain the serve. You don't have to—and shouldn't try to—kill every shot; there's no need to hit a shot with a 10.0 degree of difficulty when a simple 2.0 will suffice. That means stay away, at least on the beginner and low intermediate level, from two-wall shots and play more passes and crosscourt shots.

Shots From SSP No. 1

Generally, your strategy here should be conservative. You're 38 feet away from the front wall. The ball is dropping on a difficult angle. Kills and pinches are tough, out of the question in my mind. All you want to do is force your opponent into deep backcourt, setting up your next shot (this is a chess game, remember?). So stay with your down-the-line passes and crosscourt passes. If you're right-handed and playing the forehand, go BW 3½ to FW 3½ or BW3½ to FW2. On the back side it's just the opposite: BW ½ to FW ½ for a down-the-liner and BW ½-1 to FW 2-2½ for a pass. Just reverse the process if you're a lefty.

***SHOTS FROM SSP NO.
1:*** *In this spot, 2-3 feet
from the back wall, the
important thing is to get
your shoulders square
and your racquet behind
the ball. Stay with down-
the-line shots and
crosscourt passes. From
the backhand, as pic-
tured (#75), BW 1/2 to FW
1/2 for down the line and
BW 1/2-1 to FW 2-21/2 are
the most effective.*

2 TO 3 Feet

75

Shots From SSP No. 2

You've doubled your distance from the wall now, so let's open up our options a bit. In fact, you're now in the area of the court where our entire chapter on shot selection comes into play. Remember those six simple situations listed in Chapter VIII. You are in them. Just remember, your shots are also dictated by the distance between you and your opponent.

SHOTS FROM SSP NO. 2: In this position, along the side wall, 4 to 6 feet from the back wall, concentrate on using the shots listed in the six situations listed in chapter VIII. From here you can move the ball up the lines, crosscourt, or into the corners, if necessary (#76).

76

Shots From SSP No. 3

For BB back-wall shots, your decisions are dictated by the movement of your opponent. Some 80 percent of the time I try to isolate to the backhand side, simply because so close to the front wall your opponent's reaction time will be less (the racquet has to cross over the body, and for most players the backhand is a weaker shot, particularly under pressure). Another option here is a side wall/front wall pinch to the side your opponent is positioned. This way the ball will carom away from the opponent.

SHOTS FROM SSP NO. 3: You're 8 to 12 feet from the back wall, crowding toward the front court, so isolate on the backhand. The decreased reaction time for what is for most players a weaker shot will cause problems. Another option here is to try the front wall/side wall pinch to the side on which your opponent is positioned (#77).

⑦⑦

A final word to the wise: If you're playing this shot right, you'll most likely have to shuffle forward. If you start out beyond the 8-to-12-foot area, you'll be forced to retreat for shots and inevitably find yourself hitting behind the ball, which will telegraph which shot you're going to play. Also—and this has happened to me a thousand times—if you misjudge distance and velocity and the potential BB back-wall shot comes up short, hitting the floor and not the wall, you're sunk. So stay in that 8-to-12-foot range.

PLAYING THE SERVE OFF THE BACK WALL

Our relationship to the walls changes here. Depending on the serve, you generally want to get farther away from the side wall and closer to the back wall. Do not, however, change your basic approach to back-wall play—if the serve is above the shoulder, take it back to the ceiling; if it's below, go down the line or crosscourt. The key to playing the serve properly is your feet. They have to move. They must get you into position to put the serve in your power zone.

On a serve that hits the side wall, then comes off the back wall (a power Z, for example), you should set up 4 to 6 feet from the side wall and 2 to 3 feet from the back wall.

And what to do with a serve that slams into the back corner and shoots straight out, no telling which way it's going to go? Remember it's easier to move forward than back, so here you want to reverse the situation above—set up 2 to 3 feet from the sidewall and 4 to 6 feet from the back wall, allowing space to glide forward should the ball take an unexpectedly strong carom off the back wall.

And what about shot selection? It doesn't change. Just analyze what area of the court you're in, where your opponent is standing, and what your options are. Then execute. It's nothing more than we discussed in our chapter on service return.

11
AFTERWORD

*Y*ou will notice in this book the absence of any reference to children. Although the mechanical aspect of the game is the same for children as for adults, there are so many other factors involved when it comes to teaching the younger players, such as coaching, practice, and parental pressure, just to name a few, that I am in the process of writing a book specifically for the younger player and his or her parents.

Also missing from this book has been any instruction relating to doubles play. Again, that omission was intentional. This book is tailored for the beginning and low intermediate player, and, to be honest, I don't think doubles is the right game for such a player. With four players on the court in such a confined area, the action can become so frantic that the game can become physically dangerous for those who don't know what they're doing. If you need some extra stimulation or want to add a little variety to your weekly game, play cutthroat (three players going two on one), or better yet, make a move upward on the challenge ladder at your club.

You're never too old to pick up the game, and the best part about it is that anyone can enjoy the game regardless of level of skill. I didn't set foot on the racquetball court until my freshman year of college, and I am now in my seventh year on the professional tour. Hard work, dedication, practice, and a certain degree of physical talent have enabled me to enjoy success as a racquetball professional both on and off the court. The friends and contacts I have made as a racquetball professional will always be a treasured part of my life.

The most important point I hope you have learned from reading this book is that there is absolutely no substitute for practice. Nothing comes easy in any sport. No matter how many books you read or what type of equipment you buy, your game won't improve without practice. Next time you're sitting at home and watching a sporting event on television and you see Jack Nicklaus or Larry Bird make a shot, just remember that they have practiced that very shot both physically and mentally over and over again.

If you're serious about the game, talk to your local club professional about participating in tournaments within your area. If you ever get the chance to see a professional tournament, either men's or women's, do it. Remember, work hard, strive to be the best, and have a good time.

GLOSSARY

ACE   A serve that bounces twice before the receiver can reach it.

AROUND-THE-WORLD BALL (AWB)   Any shot that hits three out of the four walls of the court, excluding the wall behind the player's back.

AVOIDABLE HINDER   An interference that could have been avoided, thus resulting in loss of point for the player who hindered.

BACKCOURT   The court area from the short line to the back wall.

BACKHAND   A shot hit on the side opposite the hand with which the player normally plays.

BACKSWING   That part of a stroke during which the racquet is brought back behind the body.

CEILING BALL   One that hits the ceiling first, then the front wall and floor, rebounding to the back court.

CEILING SERVE   One that hits the ceiling before hitting the front wall, thus resulting in a loss of service.

CONTROL PLAYER   One who relies on strategically moving the ball around the court rather than on powerful hitting to win points.

CONTROL ZONE   The horizontal egg-shaped area in midcourt that is the key to controlling the geometries of the match.

CROSSCOURT SHOT   A drive that travels across the court after hitting the front wall.

CROTCH SHOT   Any shot that hits the juncture of two playing surfaces.

CUTTHROAT   Three-player game in which the server plays the other two players.

DEFENSIVE SHOT   A shot that is made in order to keep the ball in play and extend a rally rather than win the point immediately.

DIE   A ball that loses all momentum after hitting the wall is said to die.

DIG   To retrieve a low ball before it hits the floor a second time.

DOUBLES   A four-player game with two players per team.

DRIVE   A strong, straight-lined shot.

DROP SHOT   A soft shot that dies after hitting the front wall.

FAULT   An illegal serve. Two faults result in a loss of service.

FLY BALL   A shot that is hit before it hits the floor, including any shot bouncing off the front or side wall.

FLY KILL   Hitting a kill shot in the air.

FOREHAND   A shot hit on the same side as the hand with which the player normally plays.

FRONT-AND-BACK FORMATION (also called I formation)   A doubles strategy in which one player covers the front court and the other covers the back court.

FRONT COURT   The court area from the front wall to the service line.

FRONT WALL KILL   A kill shot that dies after hitting the front wall only.

FRONT WALL/SIDE WALL KILL   A kill shot that hits the front wall and rebounds off the side wall to die.

GAME   A contest usually of 21 points. In a match of the best of three games, the tie-breaking third game is usually only 11 points.

GAME POINT   Any point in a game, which, if the leader wins it, ends the game.

GARBAGE SERVE   A slow serve that forces the opponent into the backcourt.

GRIP   The way in which the racquet is held; also refers to the racquet handle.

HEAD   The hitting area of the racquet.

HINDER   Blocking of a player's fair route to see or return the ball.

INTERMEDIATE ZONE   The midcourt area between the control zone and the back wall.

KILL SHOT   An offensive shot hit so low on the front wall that it can't be returned.

LOB   A shot that rebounds off the front wall and travels toward the back in a high arc.

LOB SERVE   A serve that hits the front wall high and then rebounds upward, landing in the backcourt.

LONG SERVE   A serve that hits the back wall without hitting the floor first and is thus a fault.

MATCH   A competition in which the victor wins two out of three games.

MATCH POINT   A point in a match, which, if the leader wins it, ends the match.

MIXED DOUBLES   A doubles game in which each team consists of a male and a female.

OFFENSIVE SHOT   A shot that is designed to win a point.

OVERHEAD   A shot that is hit like a tennis serve.

PASSING SHOT   A shot that passes an opponent without his being able to reach it.

PINCH SHOT   One that "pinches" into a front wall/side wall corner and dies

PLUM   An easy kill shot.

POINT   A unit of scoring that can be won only by the server.

RALLY   An exchange of shots following the serve.

RECEIVER   The player who receives the serve.

REFEREE   The person who judges a match.

REVERSE PINCH   A shot that hits the side-wall corner first, then the front wall and dies.

ROLL-OUT   A shot that hits the front wall so low that it rolls out, thus making it impossible to return.

S BALL   One that hits the side wall, front wall, and opposite wall.

SCREEN   Obscuring of an opponent's view of the ball.

SERVE   To put the ball into play.

SERVER   The player who serves the ball.

SERVICE BOX   An enclosed area in the service zone in which the partner of the server in doubles stands while his partner serves.

SERVICE LINE   The line 15 feet from the front wall, behind which the server must stand to serve.

SERVICE ZONE   The area bounded by the service line and the short line, in which the server must stand to serve.

SET-UP   A shot that is easy to kill.

SHOOTER   A player who depends on the kill shot and power hitting to win.

SHORT LINE   The line 20 feet from the front wall, behind which the serve must land.

SHORT SERVE   A serve that hits the floor before reaching the short line, and is thus a fault.

SIDE OUT   Loss of serve.

SIDE WALL/FRONT WALL KILL   A shot that hits the side wall and then the front wall.

SINGLES   A game in which two players compete against each other.

SKIP BALL   A shot that hits the floor before reaching the front wall, thus causing loss of the point or serve.

STRADDLE BALL   A shot that travels between the legs of a player.

STRAIGHT KILL   A kill shot that hits the front wall and bounces straight out for a winner.

THONG   A cord attached to the racquet head, designed to be worn around the wrist to keep the racquet from flying out of the hand.

THREE-WALL SERVE   A serve that hits the front wall, side wall, and opposite side wall before hitting the floor, and is thus a fault.

THROAT   The part of the racquet between the handle and the head.

UNAVOIDABLE HINDER   When one player unintentionally interferes with his opponent while the ball is in play, thus causing the point to be replayed.

V PASS   A passing shot that rebounds off the side wall in a V path.

WALLPAPER BALL   A shot that travels very close to the side wall on the way to the back wall.

WINNER   A shot that produces a point.

Z BALL   A shot that hits the front wall, side wall, and opposite side wall on a fly.

Z BALL RETURN   A Z ball used as a return of serve.

Z SERVE   A serve just like the Z ball, except it hits the floor before hitting the opposite side wall.

ABOUT THE AUTHOR

In 1982 Dave Peck was rated the best racquetball player in the world. He is considered one of the top coaches in the U.S., has coached six national junior champions, and conducts racquetball clinics, seminars, camps, and exhibitions throughout the country. He lives in Texas with his wife.

Armen Ketejian is a writer and reporter for *Sports Illustrated.* He has written for the *San Diego Union* and *San Diego* magazine, and was the 1983 recipient of the Best Feature Story of the Year Award given out by *Sporting News* magazine. He lives in New York City with his wife and daughter, and plays racquetball in his spare time.